STREET SMART

STREET SMART

Practical skills for working with young people

John Robinson
with
Jan Greenough

MONARCH
BOOKS

Oxford, UK & Grand Rapids, Michigan, USA

First published in the UK in 2011 by Monarch Books

(a publishing imprint of Lion Hudson plc)

Wilkinson House, Jordan Hill Road, Oxford OX2 8DR, England

Tel: +44 (0)1865 302750 Fax: +44 (0)1865 302757

Email: monarch@lionhudson.com

www.lionhudson.com

ISBN 978 1 85424 903 6

Distributed by:

UK: Marston Book Services, PO Box 269, Abingdon, Oxon, OX14 4YN

USA: Kregel Publications, PO Box 2607, Grand Rapids, Michigan 49501

The text paper used in this book has been made from wood independently certified as having come from sustainable forests.

British Library Cataloguing Data

A catalogue record for this book is available from the British Library.

Printed and bound in the UK by MPG Books.

To my son,
Joel
You, your sisters and Mum bring joy to my heart and a smile
to my face every day.
My prayer for you is that you would walk close to God every
day of your life.
Love, Dad.

Contents

Acknowledgments

First, I thank God for the amazing journey he has taken me on since I have been a Christian. God has loved me even when I haven't loved myself. The day I gave my life to Christ, God stamped on my heart, "I love you, John", and through all the challenges life has brought, I know in my heart God loves me.

And thank you to my awesome family, who have lived through lots of the experiences I've shared in this book. Without their love and support over the years I could not have done the things I have. And I so appreciate the fact that they have always believed in me. To my wife Gillian, my two precious daughters Leah and Natalie and my precious son Joel, thank you for being the family I always wanted.

And thanks to Jan Greenough, without whose timely reminders I would never have got things done. Thank you, Jan, for your time and effort in keeping the book real. It has been a privilege to work with you!

Thank you to Julie Mason, who took on managing the bus ministry when God called me on. Julie has such a heart for young people and their communities. It has been a privilege to work, laugh and sometimes cry with her. The bus ministry has gone from strength to strength under her leadership.

Thank you, too, to Jon and Sarah Hobson. I had the joy of meeting them in Mossley, and they took on the Top Bar from me (Top Bar is a non-alcoholic bar for young people). Thank you for your years of friendship, dedication and hard graft.

Thank you to all those young people and their families that I had the great privilege of working with over the years. To share in their lives, the ups and downs, has been an honour and something I will never forget.

I would also like to thank my Christian family. You know who you are. Thank you for loving us all, on this massive, life-changing experience of becoming missionaries in South-East Asia. Please pray for us as we trust in God to do amazing things in this challenging environment.

God bless all of you in your journey with him.

John Robinson
jrsomebodyschild@hotmail.com

Introduction

One day I arrived at a church to give a presentation on street work with young people. As I got out of the car, I saw two boys sitting on the roof of the church, throwing stones down into the churchyard below. One of them was aiming a half-brick at my car.

"Hey, what are you doing up there?" I called.

"Who wants to know?"

"I'm John. What's your name?"

"You the police?"

"No, I'm a youth worker. But if you throw that brick and hit my car, there'll be consequences. For a start, I'm quite capable of climbing up there to join you. Why not put it down and come and talk to me?"

Five minutes later the boys were down off the roof.

Where were the church members, who were so keen to get involved with the young people on the estate around their church? They were inside, praying.

This book is for churches who want to make a difference in their communities. Its message is that prayer is good. More than that, it's vital. But if it's the only thing you do, you're short-changing God, and you're short-changing your mission. God wants to act in our world, to change lives, and he wants to do it through us. He can't do it if we're locked inside our churches, afraid to face the world outside.

As I travel around the country I meet wonderful Christians who have a real concern for the young people outside their doors. Often they ask me the same questions:

- Why is there such a distance between our church and the young people living around us?
- How can we as Christians engage with young people?
- How can we build relationships and pass on the good news of the gospel?
- How can we plan and develop our youth ministry, and what practical skills do we need?

I'm a fully qualified youth worker with seventeen years' experience of working with young people. In this book I answer these questions, and pass on the practical know-how necessary for successful street work. My message is that we can be fired with a vision to help young people, but spirituality is not enough. God expects us to use our brains as well as our hearts. That church that I visited was full of people who wanted to do something – but they didn't have the information and resources to reach out into their community with confidence and share God's love with the people around them. It's to meet their needs that I've written this book.

Chapter 1

First Things First

What is your passion as a Christian? I realized many years ago that my deepest desire was to communicate the love of God to young people, and as I became involved in youth work I realized that God had given me the gifts to do it.

I've been involved with youth and community work for a long time – since 1993, when I married and moved to Southampton where my wife, Gillian, worked. Along the way I've met a lot of people, gained a lot of experience, and most importantly, trained and qualified as a Youth and Community Worker. I've run outreach projects from a cheap, converted camper van in Southampton and from The Message's state-of-the-art, well-equipped buses in Manchester; I've worked in challenging inner-city communities and scattered rural ones; I've taught in youth clubs, schools, colleges and prisons; and I've travelled the world and seen similar work going on in America, Australia, Malaysia and Thailand. So the advice and suggestions I'll be making in these pages come from three sources: my professional training, years of practical experience, and a heart that wants to reach out to young people and show them how to meet Jesus.

I've also visited a lot of churches where people are burning with enthusiasm to go out and contact young people and take the message of God's love to them. I've given talks and presentations, and over and over again people have said, "Please give us some guidance about how to get started, how to get a youth work project off the ground."

My advice, first of all, is to get the basics right. However keen you are to get out there and start meeting people, you will store up trouble for yourselves if you rush at it. The groundwork may not sound exciting – and you may cringe at the thought of committees and management and rotas and training – but unless you are prepared to put in the time to get these things set up, you will find either that your project fizzles out through lack of support, or that your surrounding communities (and the local agencies which operate in them) are unwilling to engage with you.

Lots of people – faithful, enthusiastic Christians who trust wholeheartedly in the Lord – find this stage frustrating. "Just pray," they say, "and have faith. If God is in the project, he'll lead it where he wants it to go." That's fine, as far as it goes. I always pray for a project – it's the foundation of all I do. But what if I do nothing but pray? Who will organize the training, or make sure there's petrol in the bus, or get a million other jobs done? Yes, we'll trust in God – but he's relying on us to do our part, in the best way we can. And that means thinking things through before we get started.

I have known churches which started doing some youth work simply because they found they had money available, and it seemed a good use of their resources. Sometimes it's all worked out well – but sometimes the whole project has fallen apart because it was started with no real plan in place. So let's look at how to plan well. Faith is certainly essential to all we do, and it's important in youth outreach work: we have faith that God will lead us to the right people, and that he will change lives. But having faith is not an excuse not to do things properly!

What is your vision?

Why are you taking the gospel onto the street? I know that when I first got involved with youth work, I was driven by the desire to reach young people with the message of salvation which transformed my own life.

I have written elsewhere (in *Nobody's Child*) about my childhood, spent in foster care and children's homes. In spite of repeated efforts to sort my life out, I ended up homeless and living on the streets. I felt completely worthless, and it wasn't until I encountered Jesus – in the shape of some wonderful Christians who welcomed me and put their arms around me, dirty and smelly as I was – that I began to believe that I could be of value to anyone.

I want to share that experience with others. I want to take the wonderful message of God's love to people who have missed out on love and friendship and caring, and tell them that they matter. Unfortunately, church isn't always the best place to do it. I've found that the best place to meet young people is on their own territory – in the street or at school – where they're relaxed and more willing to listen to what we have to say.

However, it's not enough to say, "We want to reach young people with the message of God's love." That may be your ultimate vision, but how are you going to achieve it? For that, you need much more detailed aims and objectives.

Do you want to do something on a small scale – maybe a tea, coffee or soup run, that will enable you to meet people on the street? That's fine. Lots of organizations do a fantastic job doing just that. It's a real service and it opens up the possibility of all sorts of interesting conversations. There's absolutely no problem if that's your vision.

What if you want to develop this work further – do you have more long-term aims? Would you eventually like to have a building where you can operate a youth club of some kind? Most churches have premises of one sort or another that they may want to use if the young people they contact are willing to go there. What sort of work do you want to develop? A café where food is served and with speakers coming in? A coffee bar with games? With computer training? With an advisory service? (Health, relationships or employment advice are always popular, as are drug and alcohol information, but you need some professional input.) Perhaps your ultimate aim is to run a non-alcoholic bar where young people can meet their friends. Or a bus ministry like the one we ran at The Message where we had double-decker buses kitted out as mobile youth centres, with drinks machines, DVDs and plasma screens, games consoles and sound systems. You may want to specialize in outreach through sports, running a football, rugby or basketball club.

It's worth talking to other local churches and youth workers, so that you know what else is currently available (there's no point in setting up in accidental competition with a similar scheme in the next street – there's plenty for us to do for God without repeating what others are doing!) and also what has been tried (and maybe failed) in the past. You need to know your patch, and its history. What are the needs in the area that aren't being met by existing work? Don't be put off, however, if God has given you a clear vision for something that has been tried before without success: perhaps it wasn't right for the area twenty years ago, but maybe now is the right time.

Whatever your aims, you need to explore all the possibilities and work out what is feasible with the expertise and funding you have available or are likely to be able to get. You may have to start small, but have a plan for your long-term goals. There's no harm in dreaming – and God can move mountains!

Start by thinking whom you want to target – Teens? Pre-teens? Families? Then look at as many possible scenarios as you can think of. What does God want you to do? Go to him in prayer.

Setting up a constitution

From prayer to paperwork may seem like a big step. And a constitution sounds like a bureaucratic step too far, doesn't it? But actually, it's a really useful tool.

A constitution is the governing document for your organization. It defines your purpose and states clearly what your objectives are, how you plan to operate and how you are organized. Going through the process of writing all this down can be really helpful. It makes you get all your ideas down on paper in a sensible form so that everyone involved can see what you're aiming to achieve. When people see that, they can buy into it prayerfully, and give you their support because they know where you're going.

It's also a safety device: it means that the project can't get diverted from your original purpose, and it can be used to settle any disputes that might arise. It also makes people accountable to the original vision, and ensures that financial procedures are laid down so that funding is properly administered.

Having a proper constitution adds to your credibility: it indicates to other people that you're well organized and serious about what you're doing. It also enables other organizations to judge whether you meet their criteria for co-operative work or even funding.

Once you know your aims and objectives, you can decide on a name for your project. The name is important. For a start, you don't want to duplicate something else that's already established in your area. It causes confusion, and if any untoward incidents occur at the other project, then you could be affected. Be circumspect about your name –

check it out on Google and with plenty of other people before you decide on it. It's possible to accidentally choose something that has unfortunate connotations or particular local meanings you may not be aware of.

In general, your constitution should include the following information:

- the name of the project
- where it is based
- what its purpose is
- the names of the officials: a chairperson, a treasurer, a secretary to take notes at meetings, a main project leader, and many other necessary roles
- the duties and powers of the officials (e.g. you may have two people with the authority to sign cheques)
- the names of the supporters
- the frequency of meetings (for organizers as well as "events")
- the budget, and the names of the accountant and the auditor
- the policies you have in place.

I'd like to emphasize again that this is really necessary. I often come across people who say that they don't want to bother with this sort of thing – they want to step out in faith and prayer. If you are doing a one-off project for an afternoon with a group of friends from church, that's fine. It's limited and you can make up the rules as you go along – but even then, if something goes wrong, you're accountable. For a larger-scale project which will run for months or years, it's not enough. It's up to us to do the very best we can for God, and that means taking our job seriously.

We may not be "of" this world, but we certainly live "in" it, and we live in a country where there are rules and regulations. We have to work within the confines of the law, and that includes health and safety, risk assessments, child protection and all the rest of it. We have to have policies for all these things. If we are hoping to work with others in our local community, we need to show them that we have all the safeguards in place that they would expect to find in any well-run, official organization. If you are going to do youth work, you need trained and experienced youth workers as well as volunteers. Being a church and using volunteers is not an excuse for failing to do things properly. If you don't have trained youth workers in your church, seek advice. Many denominations have a youth officer with experience of setting up projects.

I've often worked in teams where we expect to spend months and months praying over the aims and objectives for a project, and getting the fine-tuning right so that we know we can proceed safely. For major projects we get lawyers and the police to look at our constitution to make sure we've got it right. It doesn't mean compromising our Christian principles: insisting on running a project that's safe *is* a godly principle.

For British readers, further information and sample constitutions can be obtained from the Charity Commission (Charity Commission Direct, PO Box 1227, Liverpool L69 3UG; www.charitycommission.gov. uk). Readers overseas should seek out the local regulations governing charities.

From "bitty" to businesslike

When I set up the Streetwise project in Southampton, I had a vision: to reach the young people in the area. I got some funding from the bishop, and I bought and fitted out an old camper van. There was a lot of interest in the project – who was this strange Yorkshireman driving round the estates? Would this project achieve anything? Would it last?

I could see that I needed support: a treasurer to oversee the handling of money, and a committee with its own chairman to whom I and my work would be accountable. Until then the project was operating but it was "bitty" – I had general support but nothing specific; I had some finance, but it wasn't clearly allocated; the work was going on but it was scrappy, there was no plan and no format.

I found a team of people to help me: some of them were the parents of teenagers, the church treasurer was a businessman and accountant who gave us his time for free, and I got some secular youth workers on board to give us advice.

We met weekly until we had formatted a constitution; we sent out newsletters to our supporters so they knew what we were doing; we contacted the local council and the Charity Commissioners; we organized signatories for cheques so all our handling of money was recorded and transparent. The work took off and gained respect from local organizations and the churches who supported us.

Outside organizations

If you're setting out to make a real difference in your local community, all these fundamental issues are vitally important. You won't be working in isolation, as one church or a little group of Christians alone in the world. As soon as you start making contact with young people you'll find yourselves interacting with everyone else – their schools, their families, the local council, the police, social services and even Youth Offending Teams. There may be local authority youth workers who are willing to get involved with your project, and you need to be able to show them that you are businesslike in what you do. Don't compromise over the fact of your faith, but don't be too proud to work with others and seek their advice.

If you know your area, understand the social issues there, and have the history of past initiatives at your fingertips – the names of the organizations involved, the statistics of their success or failure – people will be more likely to take you seriously. What these organizations see when you're out on the street, working among young people, makes a big difference. So often we've been referred to dismissively as "The God Squad", only to have people change their tune when they realize that we're properly organized, with professionally trained staff, Criminal Records Bureau (CRB) checks and everything else.

People want to know that your activities are not just for show, or done for the sake of ticking the "youth work" box on your church agenda. They want to know that your project is going to have long-term benefits for the community. That's when you start getting other organizations on board. At The Message we received funding from the local police authority, authorized because they had discovered that when one of our buses spent the evening on certain estates, the incidence of petty crime dropped dramatically – all the trouble-makers were being entertained on the bus. They didn't mind giving financial support to a Christian organization, with overtly stated Christian aims and objectives. What mattered to them was that we were making a real difference to the job they were trying to do.

Christians in a secular world

We often make the assumption that our agendas are radically different from those of other organizations – and that people are so suspicious of "religion" that they will avoid supporting a project which says openly that its aim is to spread the good news of Jesus Christ. This isn't necessarily true. My experience has been that people will listen to you – whether or not you're a Christian organization – provided you can show that you know what you're about, and you're not engaged in just a bit of aimless do-gooding. Other agencies, such as the local authority or the police, will be looking for a business plan, clear aims and objectives, a committee with a chairman and a treasurer, a regular training programme and proper provision for health and safety, child protection and so on. If those things are in place, they can see that you are approaching your project professionally, and they're much more likely to be prepared to work alongside you and support you. The work of Christian organizations is often highly respected: Christian volunteers have the motivation and commitment to make a real difference.

You should always be honest about your objectives. You may be helping young people to get into education, or housing, or employment; but if your ultimate objective is to get them involved in the local church, you should say so. In fact, if you're running the project from your local church, they'll expect it – and if you don't say so, they'll suspect that you aren't being open about your motivation.

I often used to attend meetings of the local council, and I'd hear people say, "Oh, yes, John's one of those Christians." But when they realized that I was also a trained youth worker, that I wasn't going to be a Bible-basher, but that I wasn't going to compromise my beliefs either, they were relaxed about having me there. Most people don't have a problem with that: they wouldn't ostracize someone because of their religion. I wasn't ashamed of my faith, just matter-of-fact and open about it, and I think they preferred that to someone who was wishy-washy about their beliefs.

Suppose you are trying to hire a hall. If word gets about that the event is run by the "God Squad", people may be unwilling to let it to you (and even more unwilling to attend!). But if you can say that it's a youth initiative run by a Christian organization, with full professional expertise available, and with the full support of the police and/or the local council, it's a different matter. You aren't compromising your faith, but you are at the same time providing reassurance for the owners. On the other hand, if you merely say that it's an event for young people, and they subsequently find out that you omitted to mention that you're a Christian organization, they will feel deceived.

You don't have to conceal your Christian faith and principles to set up a project that has massive benefits for the community, and gets funding and support from the secular organizations. But you do have to be open, be professional, do your homework and know what you're talking about, and build on all that.

I would also advise you to use volunteers who are sympathetic to your Christian aims and values; more than that, I usually want *all* the volunteers on my projects to share the Christian faith. Having people with different agendas on board can be confusing. People from different religions or of no faith at all may be very happy to be part of an initiative to deliver help and advice to youngsters, or to give young people somewhere safe to spend their time. But then when you want to offer prayer at the end of the evening, or give out Gideon Bibles, they may complain, and your team of volunteers starts to fall apart. Unity in a team – and certainly in its vision – is very important. This is where having that initial constitution can be of real help. Stating in the constitution that your aims are Christian means that this is clear from the outset, and people know exactly what they are signing up to.

You can say, "We are not going out Bible-bashing, but we do represent the Christian church. We're not ashamed of our faith, and we will be having a time of prayer at the end of the evening, so people can see what we do." I never had a single complaint about this during my time in Manchester, even though Sikh, Muslim and Hindu families brought their young people along to us. They didn't mind that it was a Christian project because they knew their youngsters would be safe. If it was an event where we were running the God Slot (a short talk and a prayer time at the end of the session, which we did on the buses and also in schools), they would often say that they didn't want their youngsters staying for that part. That was fine, and the project respected that. We were still giving out a good message about Christianity, including honouring and respecting people as individuals. The alternative – hiding the religious agenda and then springing the God Slot on them as a surprise at the end – would have caused enormous problems.

Rules and boundaries

Let's assume that you've decided on your project, whatever it is. The next thing to work on is your mindset. Many churches run youth clubs, either for their own young people (probably from Christian families), or for the unchurched youngsters around them. Sometimes it's more realistic to keep your outreach work separate from your church youth group, rather than trying to mix the two. In either case, they tend to have certain expectations. The unspoken invitation is, "You may join our club provided you behave in certain ways." Some of these rules may seem perfectly normal behaviour to the Christians who set them, but there may be a huge cultural gap between them and their target audience. For instance, some young people may find it very difficult to curb their swearing (they may not even notice it most of the time, it's so much part of the normal language they speak and hear), or to go for a couple of hours without a cigarette. It's easy to become very judgmental, and expect standards of behaviour which are alien to many of the people you are trying to reach.

On the other hand, it's vital that you do set down some boundaries, otherwise the whole event can get out of hand. One good way to approach this is to get the young people themselves involved in the initial set-up. Ask them questions: "What do you expect of a place where you'd be happy to come, where you want to feel safe?" This treats them with respect, as grown-up and able to make decisions. The message is, "It's your club, your place, and we're facilitating it."

However, if the adults do all the setting up, with lots of rules displayed on the walls, the young people think that someone is laying down the law, and they only know one way of reacting to that: they start to test out the boundaries. At least if they have set up the rules themselves, they have ownership of them and are much more likely to abide by them (and put pressure on those who disregard them). It's a bit like the cars in a car pool at work. They're always in worse shape than people's private cars because the people who drive them don't actually own them; so they leave them messy, they drive over bumps too fast, and so on. They don't feel responsible. On the other hand, if the young people take ownership of a project, and are encouraged to participate in setting it up, they feel responsible for making it work.

Sometimes I've asked people, "If I did that to you, would you like it?" The issue might be bullying, or swearing at staff, or swearing at each other. I point out that we ask the staff to respect the young people, and so we ask the young people to respect the staff in return. Other situations include lighting cigarettes inside the premises (illegal everywhere now), or sneaking drink in. I sit down and ask them what they would find acceptable, to make somewhere a comfortable and safe place to be.

Once or twice I've made the mistake of saying, "Would you do that at home?" Too often the reply has been a surprised "Yes." They do jump on the furniture, or fight, or smoke indoors. Then I have to say, "Well, guys, it's not acceptable here. We've talked about the guidelines and you helped make some of them up. So we ask that you respect them."

We enforce this with a three-tier system. We ask them three separate times to stop whatever the unacceptable behaviour is; if there's no response after the third request, we ask them to leave – whether it's a club night, a bus or an event. I usually say, "How you behave now determines whether you come back next week. It's not me making rules: you made them up and now you're breaking them." This puts the responsibility back on them to decide how to behave; it's not a question of you arbitrarily excluding someone, or wondering whether or not you need to do so. The limit is clear: they are asked politely, three times, and reminded that everyone has agreed on the response if they fail to stop.

Setting boundaries

When we first set up the Bus Ministry at The Message, some young people came along seemingly with the deliberate aim of trashing all our regulations. They disliked authority, and if they couldn't bend the rules, they wanted to break them. I realized that one reason was that all the rules had been set up by the adults who were in charge, and the young people resented being told what to do.

Dave was very big for his age, and he regularly bullied other kids, pushing them out of their seats and taking over the PlayStation. But when someone started calling him "Fatty", he complained.

"Well," said the leader in charge, "is it fair for them to call you Fatty?"

"No, it's horrible," said Dave.

"Is it fair that you push the smaller ones around?"

There was a pause. "No."

"So what would be fair?"

In the end Dave and the others set a new rule: "No bullying or name-calling. Everyone has to respect other people."

The effect was immediate. Dave became the best-behaved kid on the bus.

Offering the best

When you think of some youth clubs, what springs to mind? Is it a dusty hall, with shabby chairs and a battered ping-pong table, with boxes of playgroup stuff in one corner because the premises are in use the next day? Maybe the paint is peeling, and the youth workers are fed up, because all their activities are limited by lack of funds. What message does that send to young people?

Often there are real funding issues in churches. Yet there may be another youth club a few streets away in a wealthier church, maybe with fewer members – but the two don't work together and pool their resources. Surely the whole point of youth work is to operate for the benefit of the young people in the area – not to set up in competition (there will always be enough young people to go round!). It's important that churches don't just look at their own internal agendas, but explore the local area and share their ideas and resources.

As soon as you put on something for young people, whether

it's a regular club or a one-off event, their first question is, "Is it free?" Sometimes the answer to this isn't the obvious one. A free event sounds great, but what's the catch? They know society today doesn't give you much for free, and they may be suspicious. (Another case where it's better to be up front with your aims, so they don't get their suspicions of a hidden agenda confirmed when your Christian motivation is exposed.) Christian youth clubs are often free, and yet young people don't grab the opportunities they offer. And if what they offer is a shabby, damp room where debates about funding are going on all the time, no wonder.

I'm not saying whether or not you should charge for events – it depends on your funding situation. But you should think it through and make it clear at the outset, so that people know what they're getting into. Young people are astute, and they know when the people who work with them are wholeheartedly on their side, even when there isn't much money around. Often they're willing to pitch in, to pick up a paintbrush and help spruce the place up a bit. That kind of participation, and perhaps a small subscription as well, can add to their feelings of ownership.

What I would encourage you to think about carefully is just what you can afford to offer with the funds at your disposal. Cheapness may sound like good stewardship, but actually it's often just depressing. Let me explain.

What I love about street pastors and all the people who take the gospel onto the street is that they want to communicate the message of how important we are to God. He loves us. With so much uncertainty in their lives today, this is a truth that young people need to know. How can we demonstrate this to them?

Please believe me when I say that I'm not "having a go" at churches. Yet I've often been to a barbecue put on by a church youth organization, and been given the cheapest lemonade with no fizz to it and not much taste, either; the cheapest paper plates that flop when the food goes on them; the cheapest of everything. Does this really achieve our main aim, of demonstrating that the young people are important to us and to God? Wouldn't it be better to go the extra mile, spend a bit more, and see the difference?

You can buy cheap and cheerful sausages, and that's what they taste like – I call them "all snout and lips". They leave a nasty greasy taste in your mouth and you have one bite and want to chuck the rest in the bin. (Trust me, I'm not being a fussy gourmet here – I like plain, ordinary food!) The message is: "We're trying to get a result from the minimum possible outlay. You're not really worth investing in." It sounds harsh but I know it's true.

I've sat with a homeless person and bought them a sandwich – not the cheapest I could get, but a good Marks & Spencer one. Or someone's come to the vicarage asking for food and I've made them a sandwich – but not from scraps. I've made an effort: sliced some good bread, used nice thick ham, put on some lettuce and a sliced tomato. And served it on a plate, not in a bit of kitchen roll. The look on someone's face when they see that you've bothered to give them something worthwhile is amazing. It's soundly biblical, too: "When did you see me hungry and feed me?" Would you give out-of-date food from the back of the fridge to Jesus?

If you really can't manage to serve decent food at an event, don't try. If you can't afford to do it properly, you can't afford to do it. Improve your funding situation or do something else. For example, desserts done well are better than a whole meal done poorly. Don't short-change people, because God never short-changes us. He prepares a banquet for us, not the leftovers.

Suppose you go to a church event and the food is outstanding – there's proper relish and big chunky burgers – your attitude is different from the start. You don't expect it, you're surprised, you're open to what they have to offer. If people don't ignore you, they want to know your name, where you're from, little practical things – it all adds up to a warm feeling of being cared for. We want people to feel like that: that the church is here for them, ready to serve them and offer them God's love, and that we care enough to do it properly.

It's a subliminal message, but it's important: if you show you care about small things – the food, the plates – you're giving people the confidence that you'll care enough to do a lot more with the big things. You're showing them that you think they're important enough to bother about, and that's the first step to realizing that God thinks they're worth bothering about. It's about building up their self-respect and their self-image. They begin to believe that if God's people respect and care for them, God may do so too.

Chapter 2

Go Where They Are

I once started a non-alcoholic bar in the church where I was a member. I was so excited about what we would be able to offer the young people who came. And on the opening evening, with youth bands and local dignitaries all present, lots of young people and their parents turned up. It was a fantastic night – but that was it! It was like a firework: showy but short-lived. The next week hardly anyone came. It took months of patient outreach work before we had such a large group again. Why didn't they want to come?

When I was working in the Southampton area, before I qualified as a youth worker, I was commissioned by the diocese to conduct a survey to find out why young people didn't attend church. The answers I got came as a surprise to the churches I was working with, but I know that if I were to do the same survey today, in almost any part of the country, the results would be similar.

Almost all the young people I spoke to said that church was boring and out of touch with their lives; they didn't believe that the church – or church people – had anything to say that was relevant to them.

"They're all past it," said one girl. "Church is just boring! It's for people who're worried about what'll happen when they die. We're young, we're not waiting around to die."

"Anyway, we've all been out on a Saturday night," said another. "We're not going to get up early on a Sunday, are we?"

For many of them, their leisure time focused on music, sport, alcohol and their friends. They knew church people wouldn't like their music (or why would they be singing those old-fashioned hymns?), and they were pretty sure their other interests wouldn't feature, either.

So they wouldn't go to church services – but what about youth clubs, or events organized specially for their age-group? Again, they had some fixed ideas about the kind of environment that was on offer:

"Too much like school."

"They wouldn't approve of us."

"They don't smoke or drink or anything."

They felt that the leaders would disapprove of their lifestyles, dress, language and behaviour, and they didn't want to go to a place where some authority figure would be telling them what to do.

They may or may not be right about that – but it's important that we know what our image is in the minds of the youngsters we're going to meet.

This is why, whatever the project we're trying to organize, we have to go where the young people are: on the whole, they aren't going to come to us. The activities they think we're offering – sitting around quietly in church or playing 1950s-type board games – are alien to them. What we actually want to offer is very different, but they won't find that out unless we go and tell them.

"Telling them" is what motivates me. I want to tell them that God loves them, and that Jesus can change their lives, but I have to get out there and strike up a conversation first. There's no point in hanging around in an empty youth club hoping that someone will turn up. I have to go out and find them. I may meet someone who's holding a can of beer, or who has a spliff in their mouth, or who has taken a line of something or injected something: but if that's what their life is about, I want to be alongside them. It's no good waiting till they've cleaned up their act enough to conform to our church standards of behaviour, because that just isn't going to happen.

The church needs to grasp that fact. If people on the street aren't going to come to the church, we have to go where they are. I believe that if Jesus was walking around the streets today, that's where he'd be: in the bars, on the park benches, hanging out with the people on the edge of society, who sometimes do things they shouldn't, often to blot out the pain of the life they find themselves in. Sin is always offensive to God, but he still chooses to meet us where we are.

That was another thing which came out of the Southampton survey, and which, again, I recognize from my current experience: when you are dealing with young people, you find much the same social problems everywhere. This came as a shock to the good people of this part of Southampton, with their leafy suburbs and good schools and rural idylls. They thought that the problems of the inner cities were different from theirs.

Several of them had said to me, "We don't have a drugs problem around here." But I knew where the kids were smoking recreational drugs, away from the eyes of the adults, and I knew where they got them: the dealers drove there specially to supply them. Only the price was inflated, because the dealers knew that some of these kids had more money to spend.

That was the main difference – there was a bit more money around, and that could be used to mask some of the problems. Otherwise, the people were much the same as everywhere. There were families struggling to meet the emotional and financial needs of their children. The young people faced the usual problems of peer pressure, fear of rejection, boredom, and so on. In fact the problem of boredom was probably worse in the countryside because people can be more isolated.

Where they are – physically

So where do you go to find your young people? The first thing to do is to liaise with your local youth services and the Police Community Support Officers (PCSOs). These are the people who know the area: they know where the youngsters go to drink, where the different age-groups hang out, and what the local problems are, whether it's petty crime, vandalism, car theft or anything else.

The PCSOs won't ridicule you for your interest. There has been enough good, sound work done by voluntary agencies for volunteers to be appreciated. Religious organizations, schools, Youth Advisory Services, the Probation Service and Social Services all have a part to play in the welfare of young people, if poor communication doesn't hamper their efforts to co-operate. In Manchester the police used to direct youngsters who were wearing tags (electronic curfew monitors, part of the punishment imposed by the courts) to come to the Eden Buses, because they knew we could be trusted not to tolerate any trouble. We always had an excellent relationship with the local police: Inspector Steve Wilkinson says, "What I found was that where the Eden Bus was used, crime and disorder fell considerably, wherever it went, whatever the situation." (Read Steve's full account in Appendix 1.)

Don't go first to the young people themselves: they have a different perspective on the problems of their town. Instead, do your own research with the agencies, so you're armed with plenty of local knowledge. Then, when the young people say, "There's nothing round here for us," you can tell them what projects are already going on, and find out what would really make a difference. If they just mean there's nothing available that interests them, we can ask what they would like to see happening.

The other trap to avoid is copying what's already available, and maybe poaching the young people who are already involved in another church or agency's project. They aren't the ones you want to meet – someone is already helping them. You want the young people who are on the fringe, hanging around with nothing to do. That's the danger zone, where they can drift into drugs or crime through boredom.

If you were considering buying a piece of ground to build on, you'd go and look at it first. If you're considering setting up a project in a new area, you have to go and walk around it. The first thing is to get to know the locality, without approaching any young people at all. You need to know the names of places, the streets and footpaths, the buses, the shops, the amenities – everything. On the way, you'll notice where young people hang around, and you can make a note of anything special: racial groupings, changes in types of housing, anything that might be useful for your project to know. The next thing is to record all this, even if it's only a few notes. Your knowledge is being gathered for the good of your project, and you may be asked to brief someone else who joins you. (See Chapter 4 for more details on how to get started.)

So where do you go? You'll find your young people in all sorts of places: skate parks, recreation grounds, shopping precincts, amusement arcades. In the evenings they'll be outside some of the businesses that stay open late – the kebab shops and the off-licences – and anywhere that's sheltered and lit – the train or bus station, even the porches of offices on business parks. In the summer you'll find groups by the river, often tempted by drink and hot weather to dare each other to jump off the bridge into the water.

When you're ready to talk to people, tell the police what you're doing beforehand, wear an ID badge designed by your project, and don't be shy about saying that you're from a local church. That way, everyone knows you have no hidden agenda. When people get to know your face and begin to trust you, your work is begun.

Always work in pairs – preferably male and female – and know how you're going to work together. Some areas need a quick risk assessment – could you be trapped in a dark alley? If a situation might become aggressive, make sure you know what to do. Standing sideways-on to a person makes it more difficult for them to hit you, but you should have identified a problem and moved away long before it gets to that point. Never allow yourselves to be surrounded by a group. (See Chapter 8 for information on handling aggression.)

Remember:

- Survey the area (ask questions of the young people).
- Inform the police of what you're doing.
- Wear ID.
- Be open about your church connection.
- Work in pairs.
- Get some training.

The next step is to build relationships with the young people. Once you've established yourself as a regular visitor to their territory, dropping in and joining in the conversation, remember that continuity is important. They may get to know and accept you after two or three visits, but if you don't turn up for a couple of weeks, the trust will be lost and you'll have to start all over again. In between your contact times, even if you're not starting up a project immediately, it's worth being visible, shopping or walking around the area. If they see you around, the young people will probably say "Hi", and tell their mum, dad or friends who you are. Everyone gets to realize that you're part of the community and that you're there for the long haul, trying to achieve something.

In the long run, you're trying to get close enough to the young people to enable them to make informed decisions about what they want. They may tell you that they don't like youth clubs, but once they start talking about what amenities they would like – somewhere that serves coffee and snacks, with a chill-out zone and maybe computers or PlayStations – you may end up with something fairly similar. They may even surprise you and ask for organized sports. The main thing is that they take ownership of the project because it's what they've requested. Once you've collected their ideas, you'll be in a position to go to the church and explore their feasibility.

Owning the project

We once did our preliminary work in a tough area of Manchester, and established that the local kids really wanted a place to hang out and things to do with their friends. They were excited when we told them we'd be bringing the bus.

The first night there was mayhem. A wiper blade was snapped off, a window was smashed, fighting broke out and the parents came onto the street and joined in, some of them armed with baseball bats. It was a completely unmanageable situation, so we got everyone off the bus, closed the doors and drove away.

The next night we went in on foot, so there was no bus to trash. We said, "This is your project, not ours – it belongs to you. You told us you're bored, you've got nothing to do, and you complained that no one helps you. So we brought in this resource, with X-Boxes, chill-out area, big screen and café, and you trashed it. If you do that again, we'll take it elsewhere, where it's wanted."

A group of them actually apologized. Then we sat down and set out the boundaries together – no fighting, no damage to the bus, no insulting the volunteers – and they accepted them. We'd done our homework, we knew the area, and we knew these kids were seeing how far they could push us. Once we'd made the position clear, we had less trouble. (No, they didn't behave perfectly – this isn't a fairy tale!)

Where they are – culturally

Your first move is just to strike up a conversation, and you have to be led by the situation. If they're playing music, that's a starting-point, but beware of trying to be up-to-date and failing! Get clued up about the current music scene by all means, but choice of music is a fast-changing and tribal thing with young people, and you'll either be outdated by about three months or appear to favour entirely the wrong brand. It's better to ask what they're listening to and find out from them what the latest thing is.

The same goes for clothes: youth fashions change fast, often in subtle ways not obvious to older people. Never try to be one of them. Tattoos and piercings are coming back into fashion at the time of writing this book, but may be gone again by the time you read it. The important thing is never to look horrified by what you see. If you're the kind of person who can't conceal their disapproval of tattoos, low necklines or short skirts – send someone else!

You may observe some alarming activities: I've seen young people using shot-glasses of vodka which they don't drink, but use like an eye-bath. (In some countries medication is administered in this way, because it's absorbed so rapidly through the membranes surrounding the eye.) I was shocked the first time I saw someone doing that, but I had to be objective. If I'd tried to stop him, I would have ruined my chance of building a relationship, and maybe helping him with the issues that made him need the instant hit of alcohol. If you were a missionary, you wouldn't act horrified if you saw half-naked natives or people eating witchetty grubs like sweets; it's just as important not to show your surprise here. You may not have previously realized that your local park was home to a foreign culture.

Beware of:

- Asking intrusive questions
- Appearing shocked by behaviour
- Trying to be part of their culture
- Offering advice
- Trying to offer activities too soon
- Getting trapped in potentially aggressive situations.

We're all familiar with the problem of gang culture: a group of young people being rowdy, hanging around on street corners, drinking and shouting outside the shops or under the street-lamp. I try to think back to what I was doing when I was a teenager – much the same, I'm afraid. I had no parents to discipline me, and in my late teens, no home to go to other than a squat inhabited by other homeless members of my gang. In some areas you hear about almost feral groups of angry young people causing havoc with vandalism and public nuisance.

Even worse, it seems as though scarcely a month goes by without the newspapers and TV bulletins reporting the latest spate of knife crime. I wonder if it's going to get to the point where we just aren't shocked any more, but shrug and accept that this is what life's like in certain cities. We *should* go on being shocked all the time: the loss of any young life is a tragedy.

Why do so many young people carry a knife? Most of them say it's not because they intend to use it, but for their own safety – to defend themselves or to deter others from attacking them. They never seem to realize that their attacker could grab the knife and use it on them. I've had conversations with young people who clearly feel incredibly vulnerable and exposed, because no one is watching their backs for them. Maybe their dad – or their mum – is in prison, and there's no adult at home to look after them. They're managing the best they can, and they feel they have to look after themselves. Some of them are living with foster parents who try their best, but who don't understand the realities of their everyday lives outside the home – the conflicts and bullying at school or the gangs on the streets.

The world can seem a very harsh place if no one cares what happens to you. Often the young people's own understanding of what's going on may be distorted – it may not be the case that no one cares about them, but that doesn't change the way they feel inside.

In that situation, if a gang leader says, "Come and join us," they're likely to accept: gang membership brings a welcome sense of belonging to something like a family. That's what happened to me. I'd never had a family of my own, and it was great to feel accepted, to know that I had a gang of mates who stuck up for me. If I had any worries about how they lived their lives – the violence, drug use and petty crime – I buried them, because refusing to join meant turning my back on the only warmth and friendship available to me.

Recently The Prince's Trust sponsored a survey of young people, and published the results in a report, "The culture of youth communities". It suggested that in the absence of parents and other adult role models, young people turned to gangs and their friends for support and a sense of identity. It found that:

- Around a third (34 per cent) of young people surveyed did not have a parent whom they considered to be a role model.
- Over half (58 per cent) said that a key reason for joining a gang was a sense of identity.
- Almost a quarter (22 per cent) said young people looked for role models in gangs.
- Over half (55 per cent) cited friends and peers as role models.

The report suggested that young people are creating their own "youth communities" in search of the influences that were once found in traditional communities. "All the threads that hold a community together – a common identity, role models, a sense of safety – were given by young people as motivation to join gangs" ("The culture of youth communities: a report by The Prince's Trust", August 2008, Executive Summary).

When you understand the attraction of the gang culture, you begin to grasp the kind of needs the young people have – and it becomes all the more clear how the gospel we are offering can meet those needs. Knowing that you are loved and cared for and protected builds confidence and self-esteem; knowing that you can be forgiven and make a fresh start in life gives you hope; realizing that God loves you gives you the courage to leave destructive environments and break away from the gang. The church can offer healthy role models, a sense of identity and a nurturing environment in which to grow. When I was a young Christian, a godly Christian man was like a father figure to me, and he helped me to leave my past behind and strive for a future with God. He taught me that my actions had consequences – a lesson no one had taught me before. In our churches we have many godly people who can be mentors for young people – and often it is male role models who are most needed.

Where they are – spiritually

We need to meet people where they are on their spiritual journey. It's no good going in with a lot of church jargon, talking about salvation and repentance. No one will understand you.

Some people actively don't believe in God – they may have rejected everything about religion. Some may have a few ideas left over from their childhood, when God was described to them in terms a child might understand, but they've never moved on from that, so they reject the images of God sitting on a throne above the clouds, or "gentle Jesus, meek and mild". Some may have had past involvement with the church. Some may even have become Christians, but fallen by the wayside. I often wonder, who picks up the wounded soldiers? Do we talk about the Prodigal Son to them? Do we tell them that God loves them as he has always loved them, that he loves who they are right now?

It's so easy to go into an area, look around, and feel that the problems are so great that there's no hope of change. There's too much crime, drugs, drinking, violence. People aren't going to be willing to listen to you or respect you. The only way to escape that defeatist attitude is to stop looking at the problem, and start looking at the people as individuals. I loved meeting the mums and dads of the young people who came to the Bus Ministry. Sometimes they'd even come and sit on the bus and join me in a cup of tea or coffee. Quite often they'd been drinking. Humanly, I might not like the fact that at 2 p.m. they're already drunk, but they had to know I wasn't going to judge them. Once we got talking I'd hear about their personal situation, and often it involved things anyone would get angry about: loss, betrayal, loneliness, financial problems – no wonder they drank to escape the pain. All I could do was to listen, pray and get alongside them. Often they'd thank me as they left, even though I'd apparently done nothing but listen and give them a cup of tea.

Jesus told a story about a Lost Sheep, the one that goes off alone, the awkward one that strays away from the safe path – but the Good Shepherd goes after it, searching until he can bring it back to safety. Who goes after the ones who've got it wrong, the outcasts? Who goes to the places where people say, "You don't want to get involved there"? I've seen some of the most broken people give their lives to Christ on these estates, in prisons, even in police cells – once they get hold of who they are in God's eyes, and begin to understand that Jesus cares about them.

When you've got nothing, you've been told you're scum, you can't get a job, and you're struggling to pay the rent, it's hard to hold on to your self-esteem. If you're an eighteen-year-old just trying to get along, you can get sucked into the wrong kind of life because you never see anything else, and that's the way you think life is. It can be a big deal to have someone tell you that you matter, that you're valued.

I see a lot of people who say, "I used to go to church, but I don't any more. I don't feel I'm good enough." They can't live up to the expectations the church puts on them – or that they put on themselves. They feel that people in church look down on them because they've got problems. I can understand that. When I'm invited to a church as a guest speaker, I often mingle with the crowd before the event, when no one knows who I am. Sometimes someone has looked at my tattoos and nervously moved their handbag away – what does that say about the assumptions they're making? I'm not imagining it – you can tell by their nervous laughter when they realize that in spite of my accent and my appearance, I'm actually the person they invited there to teach. It doesn't bother me: I'm comfortable with who I am, and I know what God has done in my life. But I can understand why some people feel they wouldn't fit in at church.

You never know

Jamie was a hard nut, who told us over and over again that he wasn't interested in Christianity. He was a big lad and he used his strength for fighting and kicking off when he was on the bus. He was bitter about the broken home he came from, and it made him impatient with any kind of authority or anyone trying to organize him. He argued with the volunteers as well as the other kids on the bus, and regularly interrupted the prayer time with obscenities. The volunteers put up with his anger and kept on treating him with respect and patience, in the face of a lot of provocation. I never expected our relationship with Jamie to come to anything.

Then one night, just as I was pulling away at the end of the evening, I saw Jamie running alongside and knocking on the bus door. I stopped the bus and he stepped on board.

"How can I be a Christian?" he said.

I switched off the engine and prayed with him right there, leading him in the sinner's prayer, confessing that his life and behaviour were out of control and asking for forgiveness, and saying he was willing to give his life to Christ.

It taught me a lesson about never giving up on anyone, or categorizing them. God can reach places where we can't!

Fatherhood

One real spiritual issue can be the fatherhood of God. We regularly describe God as our Father when we want to convey the caring, loving, protecting, teaching heart of God. Yet the fragmentation of family life means that many young people have no understanding of this concept. Either their father has left the family, or his presence is associated only with violence, alcohol, drugs or frequent absences in prison. The word "father" isn't sweet, speaking of trust and love, but sour, reminding them rather of anger and abuse, of rejection and absence. It describes someone who looks away from a child's enthusiasm because they themselves are hurting, or because they were never taught how to respond gently and lovingly. If the image of the father has been destroyed in their lives, then how can these young people respond to the Father-heart of God?

The answer is that we have to demonstrate God's love in valuing people, taking them seriously, and listening to what they have to say. If your life reflects God's affirming love, you can show others how to relate to God's love for them.

X-Factor *values*

When I'm visiting prisons and talking to people on the street, one thing comes up regularly: the values transmitted by the culture of what's on TV. In spite of computers and digital channels, there's still a great shared awareness of what goes on in programmes like *EastEnders* and *Coronation Street*, and the competitive shows like *The X-Factor*. It makes me sad when I see young people picking up the idea that in order to be fulfilled they need superficial things like fame, money or designer clothes. I want to tell them that when we know God, we have a deeper security, and can resist the media-forced pressure to grab the things that we perceive will make us happy. They see someone on *The X-Factor* saying how badly they want to perform, saying that their talent is their life, and then the judges knock them back and say, "Who told you you were any good? You've got no talent" – and the young people identify with that.

What I'd like to see is the opposite: mentors who will get alongside young people and encourage them; who'll say, "It doesn't matter if you fail. Do the best you can. You're an awesome individual, valuable in your own right, and God cares about you. He doesn't care if your clothes or hairstyle are the latest fashion, or whether you're the best footballer or singer or dancer. He cares about *you*."

Witness

When you are going where the young people are, the most important thing is to be prepared to build relationships. There are no quick fixes in this work: gaining their trust may take a long time. You may be looking at two years before you can be accepted and get to know them properly.

My experience of working in many different environments has taught me that who I am in a community is more important than what I do. I can give money, work hard, plan all sorts of initiatives and activities, but it won't work if all people see is a human "doing" instead of a human "being".

Sometimes we've gone into an area and achieved a lot in material terms – cleaning the graffiti off the walls, picking up litter and painting the fences – and the local people are happy to accept our help, but it's had no long-term effects. But wherever we have engaged with people, talked to them, related to them, they've begun to see us as people too, instead of a faceless group of outsiders. If I reflect God, people will take notice. It's the life I'm living that witnesses to God's love, not the "good deeds" I do in the community.

Of course, this is very taxing. People will be watching us carefully, just as they watch the vicar, the pastor, the youth worker or anyone who professes to be a Christian; they want to see whether our beliefs are reflected in our lives. Whether they themselves believe makes no difference: if they can pick holes, they will. And there's no doubt that we'll make mistakes. But if we've demonstrated our fundamental passion for God, our desire to do his will, and our genuine interest in the people around us for Jesus' sake, they'll be able to judge where our heart is, and they'll forgive us.

I make loads of mistakes; I often get my Bible references confused; sometimes I've not checked out an area well enough and I've said something completely inappropriate for the circumstances. But people forgive me when they recognize that I'm doing my best and I'm fired up by the love of Christ.

So we've got to live out our faith honestly. A friend of mine gave a talk recently in which he pointed out that things are valued because of what they're made of. A watch made of gold is more valuable than a steel one; a piece of furniture made of mahogany is more valuable than something made of chipboard. Fakes are not valued. So it is with us: if we're working in a community, we're saying, "This is who I am." Am I the real thing, am I sound all the way through, or am I like a piece of wood that's rotten and falling apart? Reflecting God in a community isn't about Bible-bashing or telling people how they ought to behave, but letting them see the grace of God and the light of Christ shining in us, in the way we treat people and in the extent of our acceptance and love.

I once took a church group to a prison on Christmas Day, and the prisoners were so moved that we were there. They said, "Why would you come out on Christmas Day?" The answer, of course, was, "Because we care and because God loves you." That visit was a better witness than taking presents in, or sitting down and preaching a sermon. The Word of God is important, but the Word of God in action, in visiting them, was more effective.

So where the young people are – physically, culturally and spiritually – is where God can work and where we can witness. We meet them where they are in their lives, whether they're managing OK, or whether they need to offload their problems, whether there's been a family tragedy, or a drinking issue, whether they're aggressive and awkward or just getting on with living their life. We can't sanitize people to meet our standards, or expect them to behave in certain ways before they even believe – it doesn't work like that. Jesus said he didn't come to heal the healthy, but the sick.

But I have seen miraculous transformations. It's amazing to see the power of God at work, using ordinary men and women to share his love with the world. I've seen people who have loads of things going wrong in their lives, but suddenly coming alive when they realize that God loves them, and they understand how close to God's heart they are. That's when we can nurture their faith and equip them to go out themselves and share their own experience with other young people. It's an awesome experience, when those you've befriended start going out and befriending others in their turn.

Making a difference

Emma was immersed in the local drug culture. All weekend (in her case that was from Thursday to Sunday) she was off her face on anything she could get – cannabis, LSD, heroin. She said she was bored and had nothing else to do.

When she first came on the bus she caused a lot of problems, wanting attention all the time. Gradually she came to trust us, and recognized that we were always there for her. Eventually we let her come along as an "Associate Helper" – we had to tread carefully, because if she had actually joined the team, she would have lost all her old friends, and anyway, she wasn't ready for that. What we offered her was a subtle immersion in the team, with their core values of trust in God and love for one another.

Eventually she went off and got an NVQ in youth work, came off the drugs and became a Christian – slowly. The team's witness was highly effective: they never told her to stop taking drugs, she just didn't need them any more.

Emma said openly, "I want to make a difference," and the team prayed that the Lord would help her to do that. We watched the gradual transformation of her life. Emma is now clean, and working and witnessing among her old friends very effectively.

Chapter 3

Back to School

I have found that schools all over the country provide a fantastic opportunity for witness to the gospel. Teachers are always looking for new initiatives which educate their students and enable them to make informed choices, and if you approach them in the right way, there are many openings available. But they know that young people are vulnerable and will readily absorb all kinds of attitudes, so they will be understandably cautious about giving you the authority to enter the classroom. You must be prepared to adapt your style of presentation to work within the rules of the school. It *is* possible to do this without compromising your faith. It's a tremendous challenge, but it also has the potential for disaster if you don't first spend time building up your relationship with the school and the head teacher.

Making contact

You have to be entirely open and honest if you're going to make your relationships work. Make the initial contact with the head teacher by telephone or email, and introduce yourself as a Youth and Community Worker, or a Christian band or a church drama group, or whatever applies to you. The head teacher wants to know who you are, and why you're interested in coming into school. Once you've managed to secure an interview with the head, make sure you have everything you need (such as CRB clearance). Your paperwork and your business cards, if you have them, must look good and be professional. This isn't just for show: it demonstrates that you're taking the work seriously, and that you aren't just an amateur outfit. If everything looks shabby, cheap and slapdash, they won't want to let you in.

When I make my first approach to a school, I say who I am, that I'm a qualified youth worker and a Christian. Then I say, "If you'd like me to come in and run an assembly, this is what I'd do." It's important to tell them what you're offering – that way they know, at least, that your ideas of assembly aren't forty years out of date!

The head teacher may also ask you some questions about your job and your personal life – they'll want to get to know you before letting you loose in a school. Sadly, accusations of malpractice can be made very easily, and they need to be sure that they've made all the right enquiries about you. When I've worked in schools the head has always wanted to get to know me as a person; they wanted to have an idea about how I'd react to stress, to difficult pupils, to people attacking my faith, and how I'd deal with atheists and people from other religions. It's only if you can make it clear that you have a measured, reasoned and well-thought-out response that they'll be willing to let you loose on their students.

It's all about communication. If you're running other events in the local community, it's a good idea to invite the head and other staff to come along. That way they can see you in your "home" environment, at church or in public, and they can see how you interact with young people. If it's local, many of their own students may be there anyway. It makes a good link and a foundation you can build on.

It's also important that they know what you'll be offering. It's no good approaching a school and saying that you're willing to do anything they want. The head teacher doesn't have time to start organizing you. And do you really want to spend time every week listening to children read?

You may want to run after-school clubs. These are a popular choice, and they often depend heavily on parents and other volunteers. You might be able to run a computer club, a drama club or specific sports activities. It's a good way to get involved and become known in the school. Perhaps you'd like to set up a Christian lunch-time club, like a Christian Union. There may be children from your church already in the school, who would like that to happen. Eventually the school may trust you enough to allow you to take assemblies and RE lessons and even get involved in pastoral work.

When you're making that first approach, make sure you have a clear-cut proposal: say what your aims and objectives would be, over a six-month period (saying you'd like to see sixty conversions is *not* a suitable objective!). This will convince them that you're taking a professional approach, and this, together with your qualifications, will build confidence.

When I run an RE lesson, I don't just use scripture: I use DVDs, PowerPoint, and music too. It's a technological age, and the students expect something punchy and visual that keeps to the point and grabs their attention. We were lucky when we used the buses from The Message ministry – we had the novelty of taking the kids into a different environment. We could drive onto the school grounds and plug in the electrics, and we were ready to go. We had games and a café area downstairs, and upstairs we had front-facing seating for sixty people, with a massive plasma screen. We used to run lessons which the kids could relate to – like talking about clothing brands, and what they thought they said about people, and how we value people in our society. It's no good talking about the things that interest people of our own age-group: we've got to know what young people are thinking now, and use that to communicate the gospel to them.

The teachers used to get on the bus and have a cup of coffee downstairs, and enjoy having a break for one lesson. Then, at the end, we allowed fifteen minutes for playing on the games consoles and music systems, while we offered prayer upstairs for anyone who wanted it. If that sounds scary, I have to say that after eighteen years of offering prayer, I've never had one complaint. It's fine if people aren't interested – but often students would come and say, "Will you pray for my friend?" It's amazing how people will open up if they see that you're being open and honest, too.

Let them eat cat-food!

One of my most popular and effective lessons was on not judging by appearances, and how God knows who we really are. It takes a bit of preparation.

First you buy a tin of cat food, but it's important that it's a ring-pull can. Put the tin, unopened, in a bowl of water and carefully soak off the label in one piece – you'll want it later.

Then you get a marker and mark a line around the middle of the tin, and cut along it with a strong, sharp knife. Empty out the cat food and throw it away (or feed it to a cat). Wash and sterilize the empty can, and smell it to make sure it's really clean.

Then you crush a slice of white bread and melt three or four Mars bars (it has to be Mars – nothing else looks right). Put a big dollop of melted Mars bar in the bottom of the can, and fill with breadcrumbs. Do the same with the other half, the one with the ring-pull. Provided your Mars bar is still hot and runny, the nougat and toffee and chocolate will mix into the bread and give you a consistency and appearance that's just like cat food.

Let it cool and set, then stick the two halves of the can together with a piece of wide masking tape, stretched tightly, and cut off the ends neatly so there are no lumpy overlaps. Stick the cat-food label back on with glue, and put it in the fridge.

When you're running the class, you ask, "Who's hungry?" You get a volunteer to come to the front and then show them the tin of cat food. You ask them, "Do you trust me?" Let them open the can by pulling the ring-pull – by which time the other kids are all laughing and making sick noises: they can't believe you're going to make their mate eat cat food.

Then you give your volunteer a spoon and ask them to eat it – and he grins when he smells it and realizes that it's chocolate.

It's important not to get so caught up in the fun of the demonstration that you forget to make the point: that we judge by appearances, but God doesn't. I always say that God doesn't take photographs, he takes X-rays. He knows what's going on in your life, and he cares about the things no one else sees.

What kind of sessions?

When you're planning what you're going to offer, you must remember that school isn't the same as church. You have to fit in with what the school wants you to do, and its purposes are primarily educational. If I'm taking a citizenship lesson, I often talk about my own experiences of the care system. I can work outwards from that into topics like peer pressure, or how we fit into our local community, or dealing with life when we feel that no one cares about us. It will help if you take a look at the curriculum and find out what issues the school wants to cover.

Lunch clubs generally run immediately after lunch, and schools like them because they keep the kids on the premises and out of trouble. You need to get the students to sign in, and maybe pay 20p or 50p. This is partly because they're more likely to appreciate the activity if they've paid for it, and partly because if you provide any kind of snacks or prizes – crisps, drinks, fruit or chocolate – it all adds up and you could soon find yourself footing a large bill.

You need a name for your club, and you can let the children design a sign for the door. You need to be aware that if you start out with twenty or so students, that will probably drop down to ten or twelve. Don't be discouraged: for some of them this may be the only "safe" time in their school day. Some kids get bullied. Some will get no food all day other than the snack you provide.

As they come to trust you, they'll start talking to you and opening up. Obviously you must have female helpers for female students, and men for the male students. It's important that you keep everything they say in confidence, with one exception: if anything they say leads you to suspect any kind of abuse, you have to report it. You have a duty of care, and as soon as a student starts saying anything of that kind, you should warn them immediately that if they say any more, you will have to pass the information on to your line manager within the school. (You should have talked through the school's child protection policy with the head teacher before you started work, so that you know the appropriate member of staff to contact.)

Other activities may include music sessions (making music together or listening to it), watching DVDs, and dance or drama – anything they want to be actively involved in. Take care, though: if you put on meditative music and spend fifteen minutes praying, when you open your eyes they'll all have sneaked off! Think active, and think outside the box. Look for Christian courses for young people, but make sure they're interactive and include lots of fun. Kids don't want another heavy lesson in their lunch break.

Be sure that you have made clear session plans and get permission from a senior member of staff for what you want to do. If you're running a craft session you need permission to use craft blades, for obvious reasons. You also need to take the normal precautions you would take whenever you're in charge of young people: find out about allergies and so on – you can do a lot of damage with a peanut-laden chocolate bar. It sounds boring but it's vital. Make sure you have a trained first-aider and know what to do in an emergency. Be thoughtful: if you have a riotous session with balloons and shaving foam, don't walk away and leave the classroom a shambles – someone will have to teach in it ten minutes later. All of this is simply an extension of having a professional and responsible attitude.

What about the gospel?

So you've planned for an educational element, and a fun element, but where does the gospel come in?

A good group will have a theme running through all the activities every week. After the fun, you can set aside the final five minutes for testimony and a prayer for the students. This will be fine, as long as you set it out clearly at the start. The problems arise if you get the club or lesson series started, and then suddenly introduce prayer six months down the line. The students feel cheated, and that they've been deceived and sucked in before having religion sprung on them. No one will object if you make it clear that you're going to talk about "exploring your faith", and debate with other people about issues of belief. But if you spend any of your time preaching hellfire and brimstone, you'll never be invited back. In a good debate you don't dominate the discussion or bully people into accepting your view. You can respect other points of view without watering down your message, especially if you are simply describing what God has done in your life.

So if we do a session on prayer, we can aim to talk about why people pray and how we pray, run some fun and creative games about communicating, and tell a personal and challenging story about how

God has answered prayer. Then we could ask for prayer requests and start a book where people can choose to write their prayer needs.

It's a privilege to be allowed to meet these young people and touch their lives – we mustn't abuse it. When I share my testimony in schools, I always emphasize that it's my personal story, and I'm not pushing my ideas onto anyone else. This isn't tub-thumping evangelism, and you're not out to win arguments at all costs. Rather, you're opening up dialogue, and being there as a witness to what God has done in your life. Then the pupils will listen, because you're not saying, "This is what you *must* believe." People can always argue over doctrine, but no one can deny the fact of your personal experience.

We may know what the scripture says, but it's no use quoting scripture out of context to people who don't believe in the power and authority of the Bible. Scripture also says that we should have good judgment and discernment (Proverbs 3:21), and so we should shape our message so that our hearers can understand it. We mustn't enter a school full of our own assumptions, personal hobby-horses and strongly held views. Jesus met people where they were, and so must we.

Primary schools

Primary schools are slightly different from secondary schools and colleges of further education, because of the younger age-range and different atmosphere. My wife Gillian has worked a lot in primary schools, and she says they're often happy to accept visits from Christians, whether or not the school is a church school. They are particularly pleased to receive offers to deliver both RE and assemblies (which are legal requirements), as this is an extra strain for a busy teacher. A fresh, enthusiastic face goes down well with both children and staff.

Gillian has offered to lead weekly assemblies at local primary schools wherever she has worked, going into both church schools and ordinary community schools. She always made an effort to bring the Bible to life, talked about how everyone can have a relationship with God, and introduced lively worship songs. The children enjoyed the sessions and told her so. Often they would come up to her afterwards and tell her things they hadn't even told their teachers, because something in the assembly had touched them. One little boy said, "My mum doesn't believe in God. But I do. I believe what you said: God's there and he loves me." Sometimes, she said, you could really feel God's presence.

In one school she started a lunchtime club – she had to limit it to the Juniors, because she knew if she opened it to the whole school she'd have had all the Infants there as well. Lots of the children were keen to learn about God and were ready to go deeper than assemblies would allow. She had fifty or sixty kids in the club, and they chose their own name: Funky Prayer Warriors! It gave them a time when they were free to talk about God. There was a little opposition from a few parents who said that they didn't really want their children to attend – but then they said that the kids were insisting, so they had to give in.

Our church paid for some really good children's Bible study notes, to be given to the club members as a Christmas gift, so they could begin to read the Bible for themselves. Lots of the parents reported that the children treasured them. Years 5 and 6 made and decorated an index-card box, which they filled with their special Bible verses, and where they could write their own prayers and thoughts, as a memory box for ways they could relate to God.

The teachers were challenged, too, by the kids spending time thinking about God every week, and Gillian was available if the staff had any personal issues they wanted to talk about. One day one of the teachers said to her, "I never had much time for religion before. But after listening to your assemblies, I've decided to give God a chance. I've started going to church again." Over the years this pattern was repeated: teachers reported that their attitudes were changed by sitting in on the sessions and seeing how they helped the children, and many of them started to attend church.

Pathways to prayer

One year the school ran an RE day, with activities and exhibitions all round the school. Gillian offered to run a Prayer Event for the whole day. In the school hall she set up stations showing different ways to pray, and each class in turn came into the hall to explore everything.

There was a box of sand so the children could walk across it and make footprints. They could take away a copy of the famous "Footprints" poem.

She made a graffiti prayer wall to write on – a big white sheet stretched on the wall and some marker pens to write with.

She set out flower seeds to plant in cups, so that as they grew, the children would remember that God hadn't forgotten their prayers, and that prayers are like planting seeds in God's kingdom – the results are bigger than we think! They planted them on cotton wool in little plastic cups and watered them. Some of the children knew so little about planting seeds that they filled the cups full of water, and we had to show them how to empty them and leave the seeds just damp.

There was a table with plasticine so they could make models. Some of them did amazing little sculptures of people on their knees.

She had a book with a page in it for each of the staff at the school – teachers, head and support staff – and the children wrote prayers for them. Some of these were so beautiful that the teachers cried when they read them.

There was a quiet area with beanbags to sit on, and cards with printed Bible verses, so children could read them and think quietly about God.

She also had a table with sheets of paper bearing words about how unique each person is and how precious to God – the children could write their name and use finger-paints to make their hand-prints.

On the stage there was a gazebo with soft music playing, which became a quiet place to be with God. There was a cross, and some sticking plasters. If a child was hurting about something, they could stick a plaster on the cross, as a way of giving their hurt to God.

Who can do it?

Sometimes the best helpers are gap-year youngsters, students and people who have made the effort to understand youth culture and what it's like in schools today. If you were going to speak to a group of elderly retired people, you would study their interests; you need to do the same for school students. It's a mark of respect that you should take the trouble to know what goes on in young people's lives, understand about Facebook, Bebo and Twitter, and know what the latest things are. It's not sufficient to learn a few buzzwords – they'll soon detect it if your interest isn't genuine and you're just trying to be "cool".

It's probably easier to say who *shouldn't* be let loose in schools.

You might have to keep an eye on what your volunteers are wearing, and tell them to dress appropriately – you don't want young men in skin-tight T-shirts and jeans, or girls in skimpy and revealing tops. They're there to be good role models, and you don't want them to look as if they're on a catwalk. If they're getting the response "They're fit" or "I fancy them", then the focus is on their looks rather than on what they're saying.

You don't want people who can't stick to the script. You should have agreed with the team beforehand what they're going to say, and you don't want anyone who will go off and get side-tracked. There should be a clear understanding about what you're going to share, and it should have been cleared with the head teacher.

You don't want *really* shy and nervous people, because the kids will destroy them mercilessly, and that's the "useless Christian" they'll always remember. Use the nervous people to watch and gain confidence, and for prayer support and other important behind-the-scenes roles. It's OK to be a little nervous, because that's humbling and it encourages us to rely on God. People don't mind the odd mistake if they can see that you know what you're talking about and that your heart is in what you're saying. But if someone loses control of the class or goes off-message, the watching teachers may decide not to invite you to come again. That's disappointing for the team and upsetting for the person who feels they've let the team down. Make sure the team are included in your prayers.

What you want are people who are gifted in communicating with young people: confident, articulate people who have something to share, and a story that's powerful and to the point. You need to be able to deliver a punchy, relevant message that will plant a seed, so that the young people begin to see what God has done in your life – and would like to do in theirs.

What can go wrong?

There are a few pitfalls which you should be aware of, which apply especially to Christian groups.

First, there's the hellfire preaching. You might appear to have a great session, with all the Christians shouting "Hallelujah!" and "Preach it, brother!", but all the teachers will be saying "*Never* ask them back again!" Focusing on the love of God and how he wants a relationship with us is a much better place to begin than a theological discussion about who is going to heaven.

Then there's the problem of judgmental attitudes. I repeat: God meets people where they are, and he doesn't send us there to judge. I've been in schools where pupils aged ten, eleven or twelve get a pound to buy a pie at lunchtime – and they spend it on a single cigarette and a cheap can of beer. When the kids are sitting there in their uniforms, we don't know which ones are hungry or hurting, which ones have a mum and dad who are separated, or in prison, or on drugs; we don't know their background. We have no right to tell them that they're going to hell because of their lifestyle – it may be the only life they know, so far.

It's our job to tell them about hope, about God's love, and something different from what the world tells them. If their parents are saying, "You're rubbish, I wish I'd never had you," they don't need the school telling them they're on the road to hell. We *can* tell them about repentance in love. If we start off by telling them about all the things they're doing wrong, they won't get the message that God loves them – they'll just think that we want to tell them off, and so does God. Many of these behaviours are coping mechanisms: if we lead them to the God who heals, we will find they don't need the other things so much any more.

The next thing that can go wrong is losing the plot. You get speakers who go round in circles without ever getting to the point. Or who try to cram too much detailed theology into their talk. Or who get stuck on one point and can't remember how to move on. The outcome is always the same: the students get bored.

Once they're bored, you arrive very quickly at the next disaster: loss of control. The speaker has to be strong enough to keep order, and to say, "I'll deal with questions afterwards – this isn't question-and-answer time." You can check with a look at the teacher (who will always be sitting in the room if it's an RE lesson), and they'll support you. But once you've allowed disruptions to get out of hand, it's much harder to regain control. Again, if the teachers have to step in and rescue you, you won't be invited again.

These horror stories are only a warning: if you're well prepared and have made good relationships with the staff, there's no reason why your work in schools shouldn't be immensely fruitful.

Key points

- Be professional.
- Make good relationships.
- Run lively, interactive sessions.
- Be open about your faith.
- Be sensitive and respect other views.
- Plan thoroughly.

Chapter 4

Making Connections

If we're going outside schools and churches and into the world where the young people live, we need to have some ideas for ways of connecting with them. You may already know what you want to offer, but these are some of my experiences.

Using the internet

Over the last ten years or so more and more people have gone online. Most people use email as much as their mobile phone, and together with social networking sites, these are great ways of keeping in contact. The internet has revolutionized society, from individuals in the home to education and business. Websites are used in schools and colleges for research purposes, and young people are taught to be computer literate from the reception class at school and even at nursery.

Huge numbers of young people have their own pages on Facebook, MySpace or Bebo, making "friends" and keeping in touch. These sites allow you to join networks linked by locality, workplace, school, or common interests. They are great ways of getting your message out into the virtual world, but there are dangers: in spite of a variety of security options, all these sites can also open a gateway to abuse and bullying. There is also Twitter, a micro-blogging service which allows users to send messages (known as tweets) via a range of applications including SMS (short message service).

Online safety

There are several potential dangers in allowing internet access. The most obvious is the fact that anyone can stumble onto so-called "adult" websites carrying not only pornography but also graphic violence. My own two children love cats, but when they typed "pussycat" into a search engine, the stuff that came up didn't have anything to do with cats – a surprise for an eight-year-old. Even older teenagers still haven't seen a lot of life, and they can come across material on the internet which shocks, intrigues or confuses them. Often they don't know whether to believe what the sites say.

There are other alarming issues: suicide sites which tell people how to access drugs and guns with which to take their own lives and possibly other people's; anorexia sites which describe ways of avoiding food and encourage unhealthy body images, providing a group mentality and encouraging young people to starve themselves; there are even sites which sell attractive ringtones for mobile phones, where the person "buying" a ringtone may not realize that they have inadvertently signed a contract, and that unexpectedly large amounts of money will be taken from their mobile phone account. Of course, you'll find some young people who think it's a laugh to access some of these sites, but there are others who can be harmed by them.

One of the dangers which most alarms adults is the fact that paedophiles are known to scan chat rooms on social networking sites for vulnerable young people. Many teenagers are quite naïve about the way they use Facebook, putting their personal information on the site. Some have been known to tell their friends about a party, which sounds innocent enough – but if they haven't set up their profile properly and limited access to it, anyone can read about it. Parents have come home at the end of the evening to find that hundreds of kids have descended on their street, trashing the house and causing a riot.

These are not scare stories: we need to be wise when we're operating in this virtual world. The difficulty is that if you as a church or a youth project have given young people access to the internet, you have a duty of care. If they have downloaded illegal material (such as pornography or violent images) on your premises or through any of your facilities, you are liable; the press may get hold of it and hold you up for blame or ridicule. And in any case, you want to protect the young people from all this, while allowing the access they want, for fun or information.

The solution, of course, is to get a computer expert on your team – preferably a reasonably mature young person, who will not only know what their fellows are likely to get up to, but who can outmanoeuvre them! If you have the budget, you could perhaps arrange for them to get some relevant training, either online or through your local college, thus benefiting them as well as you.

When schools use computers, they set up a firewall system for protection, preventing the young people from accessing undesirable sites; many parents also use similar software at home. Internet access offered at any youth event will be popular, but you need to exercise the same degree of caution. Some very computer-savvy young people may even be able to turn off your firewall.

There is a wide range of protection systems around – and more will have been added by the time this book is published. At the time of writing, there are some systems you might like to check out.

For protection from adult websites:

- AOL parental controls (gives different security settings for different age groups).
- Looksmart Net Nanny (allows you to customize your settings).
- McAfee Privacy Service (blocks sites according to pre-set keywords).
- Microsoft Windows offers parental control software.
- Norton Internet Security (offers categories such as child, teenager, adult or supervisor, and includes virus protection, firewall and anti-spam protection).

For protection from spam emails:

- Choice Mail One (blocks spam before it reaches you).
- Email Protect (reports back on internet activity and instant messages).
- Spam Shield.

For protection from adults in chat rooms, the best system is to encourage the use of safe online practices: preserving anonymity, never giving any details that might allow dangerous individuals to deduce what town you live in or which school you attend. If you come across anyone who seems to be using a site inappropriately, you should try to get their username; then you can report them to the website provider who will be able to take action (information from www.broadbandchoices.co.uk).

Be SMART

We have a set of guidelines for young people when using the internet, using the initials SMART:

- **Secret.** Keep your name, address, mobile number and password secret, and never give them away, even to friends. Strangers can use these to contact you, or to hack into your computer.
- **Meeting.** Never meet people you have met online. Adults sometimes pretend to be teenagers on social networking sites, just to meet vulnerable young people.
- **Accepting.** Never accept emails from people you don't know. They may have graphic and unsuitable content or contain viruses.
- **Remember.** Always remember that people could be lying. Don't believe everything a contact tells you online.
- **Tell.** Tell your parents or carers if you ever feel uncomfortable, bullied or in danger from anything you read online.

Approach the problem prayerfully, setting up the appropriate protection and helping the young people to set up the right permissions and limits to ensure their online safety.

Benefits

The benefits of internet access can be enormous. You can put young people in touch with other young Christians, helping them to see that they are part of a worldwide movement. If you find the relevant Christian youth sites, you can reinforce the concept that faith is not just for older people: it's cool to be a Christian. Look at sites like:

- www.soulsurvivor.com
- www.crossrhythms.co.uk
- www.streetbrand.com
- www.message.org.uk
- www.christiankids.co.uk
- www.ucb.co.uk

You can get a computer-literate person to help you build your own website for your project. Locally based websites and blogs are very popular because they are so relevant, letting people know what's going on in their area. It's too easy to get alarmed by all the bad things on the internet. Why should the devil have all the best tunes – or websites? We can be a force for good, delivering fun, information and Christian teaching, if we go about it the right way.

When you're setting up your project, go back to your aims and objectives. Will an internet café play a useful role in delivering them? Why do you want to use the internet? If you can justify it, go ahead – professionally and effectively, putting all the right safeguards in place and monitoring the activity. It can be hugely successful.

Camps

We've all had those interesting experiences where we went camping and forgot the tin opener, and ended up hitting a can of beans with a brick in an effort to open it (the brick usually loses). If you can get over that, camping can be a great experience for young people: it gets them out of their everyday environment, and away from their usual resources like the TV and the computer. They have their mates around them but they can't follow their usual routines of going from the house to the park to the pub. It's always valuable to get people together and encourage them to rely on each other, and you need teamwork to put up a tent or make a meal for half a dozen people.

In fact, that's the value of any residential activity. I've taken young people from the inner city to a rural environment that's entirely foreign to them, and once they've got over the shock and started to work together, I've seen all sorts of unexpected gifts emerge. They move from an attitude of "This is my patch and I know everyone and their place in the pecking order" to one where they have to establish who's good at an entirely different range of skills. Sometimes the "weakest" member of the group starts showing leadership skills just because he's got the kind of visual and spatial awareness that lets him see at a glance where each tent pole needs to go. Taking young people away from their usual environment also gives them a special opportunity to listen to what you are saying about God without the usual distractions.

Of course, there are always hazards. The parents have entrusted the young people into your hands, and if things do go wrong the results can be disastrous, so always make sure that you have prepared properly.

Preparation

It's not just a case of saying cheerfully, "Let's just load up the van and go."

First, make sure that you've got all the paperwork you need. That includes written permission from the parents or guardians for the activity you've planned to do, home contact information (addresses and phone numbers) and all things medical: information about medication and also about allergies, asthma and so on. Always plan on going somewhere where you know you can get a mobile phone signal for your network – you never know when you'll need to make that emergency call.

Make sure you take the right things with you (not just the tin opener): if you don't have a lot of camping experience yourself, take someone who does, and get them to help you make the lists of what you'll need. Have you got a budget? Camping's cheap, but you still need the basics, and more than that, if it's to be a reasonably comfortable experience for everyone. You can buy a mini-fridge which charges from your vehicle, which avoids the runny butter and semi-solid milk problem. You need matches (preferably the sort with wax round them so they don't get wet), camping stoves and gas (unless you're planning to be really hardy and light campfires – not recommended!), cooking equipment, tents, groundsheets to stop the rain getting in under the tent, pillows, sleeping-bags, suitable waterproof clothing, changes of clothing, cameras, a first aid kit, toilet paper, toothpaste, sanitary towels – the list seems endless. Some of it you will expect the young people to provide, but you need spare supplies of most things. For some reason they always forget things or run out, and they often don't realize that when you're in the middle of Dartmoor you can't just nip down to the shops. It's difficult enough when you're taking them out of their home environment; it helps if you have the physical basics covered.

The other thing is to take the right people with you. Child protection issues are even more important for residential events: take only CRB-checked individuals, and make sure adults never work in one-to-one situations with young people. You need people on your team who can cook, and produce a decent meal for hungry youngsters under tricky conditions; you need people who are good at putting up tents (if you don't check the young people's efforts, several tents are likely to collapse in the night or blow away in the wind); and you need mentors who will be alert to the stresses the young people will be under when they face the challenges of the camping experience. Before you even start planning, you need to pray for the right people. And once you're ready to go, pray again, for good relationships between your young people. Ask God to work through the event, and sit back and watch him do amazing things in their lives.

Two weeks before you plan to go, hand out checklists of what people will need to bring (pillows, sleeping-bags etc.). Two days before departure, hold another meeting and check that they've got specific items. The worst thing is to drive for 200 miles and then find that people have missing equipment. On the day, no one comes who hasn't handed over their signed permission slip.

What can happen?

The answer to that question is "Just about anything – both good and bad." I've never had too many problems, just the usual things you'd expect: youngsters who are unexpectedly homesick; finding a group of them having a fag round the corner or behind a tree; having to search bags to check for drugs and alcohol; and finding that the boys have all brought contraceptives with them because they've only come for one thing.

More demanding are the emotional difficulties that arise as people come out of their shells. Once they've been living with you twenty-four hours a day for a few days, trust begins to develop. In this new and different situation they begin to open up, and tell you things they've never told anyone. It can make them extremely vulnerable.

Over the years I've seen hundreds of young people give their lives to Christ after camping at places like Lee Abbey or Soul Survivor.

Sometimes those events have started by being really difficult: I've taken alcohol off the young people, and woken them in the morning and found them still drunk. They've gone off and picked fights with other people on the campsite, and I've been very grateful that I found out whether anyone had brought a knife along, and got them to put it in a locked box. Then they've gone to the seminars and met young Christians and read the Bible, and I've watched them come alive – even their body language and their facial expressions seem to change.

You have to have the ability to stand back from everything that's going on, and keep calm. You need to be able to accept them and their difficult behaviour without being judgmental, but at the same time give them firm boundaries. God is in charge, and we can trust him, but he gives us the wisdom to care for and protect these young people and keep them safe. It's great if the whole event goes off peacefully and nothing happens – but it's vital that you're prepared for anything.

The important thing is never to lose your rag: they always know which buttons to press, and they'll bait people and try to get a rise out of them. If you persevere with patience and love, change will happen. It's worth it, if only one person gives their life to Christ; if only one person makes a small change, learns to value themselves and stops self-harming; if only one person starts to feel that they have a place in the world, in the space you've made for them to find that out.

Be firm but caring

I once took a group of young people to Lee Abbey to camp (I told the story in *Somebody's Child*). The journey to Devon from Manchester was a nightmare: I had to keep stopping the bus to get the young people to put their seat-belts on, because I couldn't drive them anywhere without them. We stopped in a service station for more petrol and I found one lad urinating in a rubbish bin, to the horror of other customers. I had to explain to him that they had toilets there. When I tried to take away the vodka they'd brought with them, they drank it all first and refilled the bottles with water, so most of them were very drunk. We had to set boundaries for their behaviour. But by the end of the weekend, they'd begun to get over the culture shock of being asked to stick by the rules. Some of them were deeply affected by the testimony of one girl who spoke to them, and later several of them gave their lives to Christ. When we talked about it afterwards, they said that what had influenced them most that weekend was the way the leaders behaved: never shocked, always caring, but firm too. I think it made them feel safe.

Non-alcoholic bars

Non-alcoholic bars are a favourite activity of mine. In Europe and the USA there are plenty of cafés and bars open in the evenings where young people can go for coffee, soft drinks, cakes and so on, and just "be" with their friends, with less pressure to drink alcohol. Offering them a similar environment, which is attractive enough for them to want to spend time there, can teach them that it's possible to have fun without getting drunk.

Plan ahead

Once again, the secret is good planning. First, think about the setting: it's no good looking for a room you can fit twenty people into, just because you think you know about twenty young people who might come. You need to think long-term: if your bar is going to grow, you need to see the potential. Setting up in premises that are too small is no good – it's like kitting out a bus with all the latest gadgets and then finding that the chassis and bodywork are rusty. If you're going to start a bar, think bigger.

Look at different venues: a church may be OK (it will help the young people to learn that they have to respect a building where people worship), but you need to see how much space is available exclusively for your use. You also need to think carefully about whether the premises will be rented or bought. If you have the finances, it's good to buy, because then you don't have to worry too much about how the place is used the rest of the time. If you have to hire, lots of organizations have big buildings standing empty (e.g. warehouses) which they're prepared to rent for a minimal amount.

Once again you need a team: try to find a group of young people who share your vision and will sit down with you to do the planning. You may not want to call this group a committee, because it sounds too stuffy, but that's what it'll be. You need their know-how about what young people find attractive, and they need your adult ability to organize and make things happen.

You'll need to pray for the finance, and maybe inspire your fund-raisers with your vision. The team who will facilitate the running of the bar must be willing to commit themselves for at least six months to a year: it's important to build relationships with the young people, who will want to see the same faces around. Your team should have complementary skills – not everyone can do everything – but you do need stability. The best bartenders are young people whom you've trained to manage the bar and operate it, but you also need astute adults around who can keep an eye open for drugs or alcohol that are sneaked in, and to prevent theft.

Go and look at ordinary bars which are popular with young people – what (apart from the alcohol) attracts them? What's the décor like? If you're planning the layout, where will the chairs be? Sofas and bean-bags can work, but if they happen to be even slightly shabby, you could be back to the old, scruffy youth club image again. Put proper sofa-style seating around the walls, and set out tables and chairs – can your bar comfortably accommodate enough people? You'll need to design the interior, and get the services of a painter and decorator, and probably a joiner, too, to make your counters, and a plumber to install sinks for washing up.

Put a really big mirror on the wall behind the bar for the shelves and bottles of syrup, which is what you'll be using to make the exciting-sounding cocktails you'll be selling. There's a company called Arcade (Amethyst Resource Centre for Alcohol and Drugs Education – see www. amethyst.org.uk) which supplies everything you require: alcohol-free cocktail mixers, cocktail shakers, straws, parasols, drip mats, pourers and recipe cards.

Difficulties

As with all activities involving young people, you have to be alert to possible difficulties. You don't want to get loads of people hanging around outside your bar, smoking or hiding drink in the bushes so they can come out and have a swig when they want. If the place attracts a lot of youngsters it's likely to happen, and you need to stop it straight away. If your bar is on church premises and the congregation finds the grounds covered with sordid litter – used contraceptives, syringes, cigarette ends and empty bottles in the bushes – no one is going to buy into your vision for taking the gospel to the young people in the area.

In that case you have to explain it to the church – that you are meeting people where they are, reaching people who would otherwise never come near a church. Through your bar maybe 50, 100 or 150 young people may be hearing the gospel each week, and enjoying an evening that won't end in a drunken brawl on the street corner. You will only be able to make a non-alcoholic bar work if your church is behind you and you have enough adults who share your vision and are willing to work with you.

Publicity

Of course, first you have to reach your young people and tell them what's available, and that means publicity in the widest sense. Make connections with all the local youth clubs, schools and youth agencies, both secular and Christian. Set up a big launch party and invite the mayor, the head teachers of the local schools, the uniformed organizations like Scouts and Guides, and the managers of other youth projects. Make sure that other youth clubs don't think you're trying to "poach" their clients: you're offering another resource, something no one else is offering, which will add to their provision in the area. Write a press release and invite the local radio and newspapers to cover the event, and generate some free publicity that way. The aim is to make a splash and ensure that the young people in the area know you're there.

What's the point?

There are dozens of activities you can run at your bar: pizza nights, quizzes, curry evenings; you may even be able to set up a big screen for people who want to watch football; but there must always be a Christian message at the end, or it's just a bar. For the volunteers, the best part of the evening is the discussion at the end. It's important that it's structured and everyone knows it's happening – not something optional that happens in a quiet corner that people can ignore. No one has to attend (they can always leave) but the business of the bar will stop then, because this is the point of the whole evening. We mustn't be ashamed of it. If you include a Christian message every evening right from the start, there are no surprises. If you set up your bar and introduce it later, people will think it's a catch, that you got them there under false pretences.

For the same reason, you should be open about your Christian faith from the start. Have a place to display Christian literature, posters and leaflets, and have Bibles around. If all the leaflets are dog-eared and stuffed in a drawer somewhere, the young people would be right to wonder how important our faith is to us. But if we make it clear that this is why we're here, and that we'll make time for a testimony or discussion at the end of every session, they'll understand. You might think they'll all just leave, but usually most of them stay. Personal stories are always gripping, and if your members are prepared to talk honestly about their own lives and faith journeys, it can be riveting. In addition, the young people observe your actions, and they'll see from the team's manner – the way they care, pray, respect and honour each other – that their faith is important in their lives.

I often think that we make evangelism hard work (and frighten off some of our more timid church members). It doesn't have to involve Bible-bashing, laying down rigid rules of behaviour, or deep theology. Scripture tells us that faith is a decision we have to make for ourselves, so it doesn't make sense to try to stuff it down people's throats. If we live out our faith, our lives will be our witness. This is why it's very important that all the adults working alongside us must be Christians: you only need a few people who may like the idea and be willing to work with you, but who don't share your Christian vision, and you'll see the effect of your witness slide away terrifyingly. You need a united team who can gather in prayer to support each other.

An outreach project whose purpose is to help young people to know Jesus needs back-up. The youngsters need a church fellowship ready to receive them, and a discipling group such as a Youth Alpha course ready and waiting. Just being involved in the project won't be enough to help them grow as Christians.

Bus ministry

Bus ministry is not for the faint-hearted or for the hard-up! My model is the Eden Bus Ministry run by The Message in Manchester, which was blessed with excellent funding and was able to build well-equipped buses. You may think that you can't possibly do anything on a similar scale, because good technology costs money. I'd encourage you to do two things: first, pray and explore all the options thoroughly before giving up. Find out who will give you discounts, who will give their time and talents free, and so on. Consider what things you can do without while still making your bus attractive and professional-looking; if all you can offer is a coffee-machine and a place to sit in the warm, will anyone be interested? Secondly, if you decide you can't afford to do things properly, and provide up-to-date equipment (and maintain it) in a high-quality vehicle, then seriously consider giving up that dream and doing something else. Otherwise you'll be back to the mobile equivalent of the scruffy youth club that no one attends.

A bus ministry is a great resource, but good preparation is vital, or you can do more harm than good. You're going to need the finance for buying it, but also for a professional paint job, graphics and décor, the fitting out, the equipment, and the fuel. But if you buy a vehicle in haste and find that it's a heap of rust that can't be salvaged, you're wasting your money (and it will cost even more to pay for its disposal). If you try to paint it by hand and it looks a mess, no one will want to use it. So lay your plans and do your budgeting with care.

I must emphasize again: this is not spending for the sake of it, it's not poor stewardship or wastefulness, and it's not just about "appearances". God looks beneath the surface and sees our heart and our intentions, it's true, but young people don't. If it looks like a scruffy, make-do-and-mend outfit, they won't be interested, and you'll have wasted what money you have spent. Buying good equipment and paying for a slick image is not about making yourself look good, it's about the young people's self-esteem. If they see that you think they're worth that kind of investment, it's the starting-point for understanding that God thinks they're worth something, too.

The value of a bus ministry is that it makes it possible for you to take Jesus out of the church and onto the street. It's a youth centre on wheels, enabling you to reach places and people you would never reach otherwise, and young people who would never come to a youth club, no matter how good the facilities. You can go into the really rough areas, knowing that if something kicks off you can just drive away, keeping your volunteers safe, but also giving the clear message that unacceptable behaviour results in withdrawal of the facilities.

Making a bus ministry work is all about making connections. You need to make good contacts in each area you want to visit, ideally finding people from that area to join the team. People need to know what you're about, and you need to be patient: it can take up to two years to be accepted into a community. Find out about local events like football tournaments, and get to know the people who run them. Then you can get permission to take the bus there: we used to take the Eden bus to parks and stadiums as well. Equipped with Christian flyers, Bibles, DVDs and support groups who will be praying for you, you can contact hundreds more people. There are not many mobile churches who can drive around and take the gospel onto the streets. Our ministry was so successful that we not only had the encouragement of the local police authority, but also financial support from them. They had a budget for reducing crime, and the Eden buses, by occupying some of the worst troublemakers in the area, were an effective way of doing that!

Practical issues

It's vital to be aware of the practical issues: you can't just drive up and park and run the project wherever you like. Always get permission from the council to park the bus and operate it. Buses are heavy vehicles and there may be weight limits in some places; when a crowd gathers the police may move you on for causing a disturbance if you haven't already liaised with them about parking.

Is your bus taxed? Has it passed the MOT? Have you had the emissions checked? Are your drivers trained to drive a vehicle of the appropriate weight? What about health and safety issues: are there any tripping hazards? Are all the electrical systems safe? Do you have a first aid box and a member of staff who is trained to use it? Have you installed CCTV so that you can see all around the bus to monitor and record any incidents?

If you have DVDs, PlayStations, X-Boxes, or Wiis, are they all secured and locked? If you have a café area, do you have hot water to make hot drinks? (Hot water can scald if it's thrown when a fight breaks out.) If you have a vending machine for soft drinks and chocolate, is it secure and encased in safety plastic? After a couple of "accidents" we had our giant plasma screen encased in toughened plastic, too.

If you and your committee think through all these practical issues prayerfully and take the appropriate steps, you are much more likely to make a success of your ministry.

How it works

However much you spend on your equipment, your biggest asset will always be your volunteers, whether they're working directly with the young people or supporting you in the background. You need a team of people: the bus won't drive itself, and your drivers must all have the right training. It's a job that often suits people who may not want to get too involved with the outreach, but can be relied on to keep an eye on things while everyone else is busy.

When I operated the bus ministry we had a general pattern for a typical night. First the team met and prayed together, then drove to the work area for that night and ran the session. At the end we closed up the bus and drove off, then stopped for a debrief and more prayer before garaging the bus and going home.

We always prepared carefully for every session, making sure that everyone was aware of local issues (whether these were recent events in the area, the names of anyone who was barred from the bus, or just young people with particular problems). We allocated volunteers to specific areas – four upstairs and four downstairs, in mixed male/female teams. Once we arrived on site, we opened the doors and the kids got on. Some played with X-Boxes and PlayStations; we might show a film or listen to music, or they might just sit and have a soft drink and talk to their friends. The staff were alert all the time: they didn't allow people on the bus if they had obviously been drinking or taking drugs, and they kept their eyes open for guns or knives. They were all trained to use minimum force to defend themselves. We did occasionally find ourselves in scary and potentially violent situations, and we were glad of that training. Mostly we sat and chatted with the kids about anything, not necessarily religion: just being there was our witness. We made sure they knew we were Christians, and they saw us acting like Christians. They knew we prayed on the bus, and we weren't ashamed or embarrassed to explain why.

At the end of the evening we always had an explicit Christian message, and again we didn't make anyone stay, but they weren't given the option of continuing with what they were doing. Either they joined us for the God Slot or they left the bus. Someone would share their testimony – not telling them what to believe, but just saying, "This is what happened to me." Mostly the kids loved hearing people's stories. Then we answered any questions and had a time of prayer. It was surprising how often the young people would ask us to pray for them, or their families.

A bus ministry is a tremendous opportunity to share our faith – but like every other activity we've talked about here, it needs to be approached professionally and you have to make links with the local community. Then you can begin to open doors to the gospel.

Chapter 5

Outreach Strategy

One of the most important tools at your disposal is preparation. Whatever the activity you're planning, whatever the group you're hoping to reach with your message of God's love, preparation is vital. It won't substitute for enthusiasm and energy and goodwill and staffing and finance and all the other things you need – but the lack of it will certainly sabotage any project, however well endowed it may be with all those other things. It's never any good just to decide on a course of action and blunder into it. You need a strategy. This chapter will show you nine vital steps to making your project work.

1. Assess the area

If your local council is planning to build a new leisure centre or park or shopping centre, it doesn't just select a site with a pin and tell a construction company to start building. It commissions all sorts of research projects to find out who lives in the area, and what the people want and need. It does its homework and preparation before making any firm plans. So should we.

Get a map of the area and study it. Look for the youth facilities (if there are any), but also be aware of the location of parks, shops, public toilets, schools, and any areas that will be well lit after dark. (How often have you driven through an area and seen a group of young people hanging about near a streetlight?)

This is important not just for knowing where young people might be, but also for down-to-earth reasons of personal comfort and convenience. If you're going to spend two or three hours in a location, you're going to need access to toilets. It's not just your team who may want to use them: if you're somewhere with no loos nearby and more young people come along to see what's happening, you'll find the blokes using the bushes or people's gardens – not a good way to introduce your activities to the local residents.

A look at those lit-up areas will often give you further insight into local people's lives. In many housing estates, the only lit areas contain a pub, an off-licence and a chip shop. It tells you something about the choices your young people have available.

Getting to know the area will give you the answers to lots of practical questions. Where will you park your car or a bus, if you have one? In some places, if you park your car on the street, there's a high likelihood that when you get back to it to drive home you'll find it's been damaged. My car has been broken into on several occasions – admittedly the kids involved didn't know it belonged to me, and I didn't know the nature of the area I was working in at the time, or I would have been more careful. (And nowadays I never, ever, leave money or valuables in the car.)

Not all this assessment of the area happens on foot. Go to local vicars who have been living and working in the area for years, and contact other people – pastors, police, youth workers, teachers and the Youth Offending Service. Doctors and nurses won't break any medical confidences, but they can tell you what issues are significant: which drugs are on the street, how much of a problem underage drinking is, what problems fill the Accident and Emergency department on a Saturday night. The police can tell you whether it's a burglary hot-spot, or whether shoplifting is a problem; whether there's any gang culture, knife crime, or joy-riding going on. It's important to get a picture of what goes on at weekends, when you get the highest numbers of young people on the streets.

This assessment is important because it's vital that you and your team know the place you'll be working in. God already knows what's needed, and we have to be open in our prayer time to catch his vision, and have the passion to work it out and see lives changed. We can do that more effectively if we know what the opportunities and problems are.

2. Meet the people

It can be dangerous to march into an area without meeting the people first. They tend to resent "outsiders" coming onto their patch and appearing to tell them what to do and how to live their lives. We don't want to be seen in that light. We want to show people that we are willing to get alongside them and help them to help themselves.

A good starting-point is a questionnaire. Ask what there is for young people to do, and what facilities there are for families. Generally you'll find that there's a park, but if it's mainly hard surfaces, littered with broken glass and used syringes, you wouldn't want to go there – and neither will the families living nearby.

Ask what the local problems are. Is vandalism an issue? You may have noticed graffiti sprayed on houses, shops and walls. In areas where there is lots of empty or derelict housing, there may be burned-out houses, and sometimes cars, too. Sometimes people don't go outside much, even in summer, but stay in their houses because there are gangs of young people roaming around the estate, breaking windows, throwing stones and shouting abuse.

Ask what facilities they would like to have: a youth club, a non-alcoholic bar, or even just a lit-up area. In one part of Southampton we found that all the young people wanted was a big umbrella they could sit under, to meet and talk to their friends and have a cigarette. (Of course, some of the cigarettes turned into spliffs, and occasionally some of the meetings involved some anti-social behaviour, but there were plenty of young people who really did just want a place to hang out with their mates – a safe place.) Other suggestions included a skate park, some after-school clubs and even army cadets!

If you don't ask the people you'll never know what they think is important. You could come up with some great ideas, but they might turn round and say, "That's your idea, not ours." It's OK to make suggestions for them to consider: they may never have thought it was possible to have a bar that looks and feels like a really good pub but doesn't serve alcohol. You may get some silly comments on your questionnaires, but you may also get some amazing ones.

I can't stress enough how important it is to meet people. I don't want to sound like a politician when I say, "Hear the voice of the people in the area," but didn't Jesus go where the people were? Don't we, as a church family, also need to go where the people are and meet them, before we can reach them with God's love?

3. Establish the history

You need to know the history of the area you'll be working in. What has gone on before? Your area may have a history of drug-dealing or gang warfare; you need to know. Some events cast a long shadow – suicides or murders affect people who may not even know who was involved, but they feel the whole place is somehow tainted by danger or cruelty or despair. I once worked in an area where several racially motivated murders had taken place many years before. I assumed that it had all been too long ago to matter, but the local awareness of that history inflamed racial tension every time it erupted. You might say that every city has a history that includes drugs, alcohol abuse, violence and prostitution at some time, whether recently or in the distant past. But the past affects the present, both historically and spiritually.

You also need to know what projects have been started (and perhaps have failed) there. When you talk to local ministers and youth workers, find out what has or hasn't worked before. There's no point in going to a lot of trouble setting up something that the young people have seen before and either ignored or rejected. Of course, you can always take the germ of an idea and realize it in a different way – but you need that basic information.

Consult the people on the ground and take their advice on board – or else they'll just be watching and waiting for you to fail. I once spoke to a vicar who said, "It's great, what you're doing. But we've seen so many people come here with good intentions. They raise the hopes of local people, and then they leave. It's better to go away without doing anything, than to start something that fizzles out, and leaves people in the lurch while you go and start all over again in a different place."

He's right. Sometimes the setting up of a new project can be very exciting – perhaps the most exciting part, when all your helpers are fresh and optimistic. It's staying there for the long haul that can be hard, on the days when it's wet and cold on the streets, or not many young people seem interested, or when your message seems to fall on deaf ears. It can be so tempting just to throw in the towel and say, "It's not working. Let's try this somewhere else."

That's when you have to hang on to the vision that inspired you in the first place, and that's when you need your strategy to hang on to. You don't want to set your hand to the plough and look back – because if a ploughman keeps looking over his shoulder, he drives a very wiggly and uneven furrow, or even goes off-track completely. You need to keep your eyes on your goal, specifically on the aims and objectives you drew up in your original vision document.

4. Share the vision

That original vision may have been yours, but for a successful project you need to share it: you need to inspire the local people who will be the backbone of your activities.

Communication is one of your key strategies: getting to know the people in the area, and not being ashamed to say who you are and what you're doing there. As you walk around the town and meet people, be brave enough to say that you're a Christian and you want to see God do amazing things there. You need to be visible, because it's who you are in a community, not what you do, that matters. People are drawn to you when they see that you have integrity, vision and a passion for your faith. With God we can do great things. But if the work isn't anointed by God, it won't last and it's unlikely to bear much fruit.

We believe that God answers prayer. We need to go out into the local churches and get them praying. They will want to know what you're doing, and they won't want to see you riding roughshod over whatever initiatives they've already got in place, and the projects they have worked hard to establish. That's why you did your assessment and established the history. If you keep them in the loop and consult them, they will be willing partners in prayer, and probably in many other activities too. If you can share your vision with the local churches, you will gain access to a huge reservoir of time, talent and prayer power. Even if you're unable to work together for some reason, at least keep all the other churches informed, so they know what's going on and can support you in prayer. As Christians, we are never in competition.

The same goes for all the other groups of interested people in various organizations. If they aren't Christians they may not share your faith position, but they can share your vision for change. There's no need to hide the fact that you are a Christian organization, but you will have to prove your professionalism to people like Social Services, the Youth Offending Service, local councils and the police. But once they are convinced that you are taking seriously the issues important to them, they will be ready to accept the fact that you want to help local people, and bring God into the equation as you do it.

In some places where we've taken the Eden buses, we saw crime go down by a third, and that was recognized by both the local police forces and local government. But we established good relationships from the outset because we included the police and local councils in our communications. They might not know much about Christianity – they might even think we're a bit weird and wonderful, with our insistence on prayer time and the God Slot – but they get over that when they see that we're honest, that we can demonstrate common sense and professional attitudes to our work, and when they see the results. I don't mind being thought a bit weird if I'm doing it for God. It's not an ego trip I'm indulging in for my own benefit; I'm doing it for the benefit of the young people and their families. I've got a very serious purpose, and that is to bring real hope into young lives.

It's sharing the vision that makes the difference. We can go into areas where there is deprivation and a lack of hope, where people hide away for fear of crime, where the place looks run down because of burned-out cars and burned-out lives, and we know that prayer changes everything. Sometimes we have prayed for weeks on end, and then suddenly we see a breakthrough. People come and say, "I don't know what it was, but something happened the other day and I started thinking about God…" You know it's God in action.

When you share your vision, you have the opportunity to inspire local people and the youth workers (if any) already working there, but you have to be prepared to stand out from the crowd to do it. Sometimes those already working in an area feel threatened by new initiatives, as though you are saying that what they are doing isn't good enough. It's worth spending time building relationships in order to avoid this. You also have to be proactive, so that if people see you out and about in the town, they recognize you. If you happen to be praying, don't worry that they'll think you're strange. If they trust you, they'll respect you and know you're not ashamed of your faith. People may have lived and worked in an area for a long time and been worn down by it; they need your vision, energy and passion to start making things happen.

Vision brings hope

I once went into a youth club on a really run-down estate: there was graffiti all over the outside, the windows had been broken and patched with wood, and it was scruffy and battered. I met the Christian youth worker there and he was despondent. I breezed in with all my hopes and aspirations, and he showed me his budget: there was nothing in it. There was no money for new sports equipment, no money to take young people out on trips, and certainly nothing to make repairs and do the place up. None of the local agencies or charities was able to support him, though he had applied to a lot of them. No wonder he was disillusioned: he felt as if he was pushing a weight uphill with no help.

We sat and had a coffee and prayed together.

"Let's do some fund-raising from the local people," I said.

"John," he replied, "the people round here haven't got any spare money."

"Maybe not," I said, "but what little they've got they'll give to invest in their own area."

We ran a football tournament (that always goes down well) and a barbecue. We asked a local businessman to fund the food, and we made sure it was good quality. Some of the girls did face-painting, and at the end of the evening we had a disco. We raised enough money to take the young people out for the day, and involved some of the local families.

It all made a massive difference to the club, to the local sense of community, and to the leader. I hadn't actually done much, except to have a vision and share it, and have the energy to help put it into practice.

There was one occasion when we were due to take a bus onto a housing estate and it broke down. We could have just cancelled, but we didn't.

We couldn't drive there so we went on foot, and had our regular prayer time before "opening up", standing in a circle on the pavement in the pouring rain. Curtains were twitching all down the street. But afterwards, when we were standing chatting to the young people who arrived, they were hugely impressed with the fact that we'd promised to be there and we were. We thought they would be disappointed that the bus wasn't available, and they were, but they were delighted to see us, just the same. They were fascinated and inspired by the dedication that kept promises.

Whenever we start work in a difficult area we need to hang on to that original vision that inspired us, and share it with others. Remember, God could do it all without us – but he graciously chooses to use us. I want to be used by God. Who will stand in the gap, and stand up for God in communities where people say, "It's just an awful place to live, there's no hope"? We can make a difference if we inspire people with the greatest hope of all.

5. Spiritual mapping

What is spiritual mapping? It's the next step after getting to know the place and knowing the history. You've found where all the painful and dangerous and despairing places are – it's time to claim them for God.

First you need to call to prayer all those people who have a vision and a heart for the area. Go into the churches and tell them what you're doing, and ask for their help. Hire a room or borrow a church, and ask those people to intercede for you and the place. Surround it with prayer. People will grasp your vision all the more readily if they have been praying for it.

Then take your team, and walk round the areas where there has been trouble in the past, like the places where young people gather at night; the pubs where fights happen regularly; the corner of the street where the drug dealers live. Go in groups of two or three: if there are twenty people in your team and they all come with you, it can be intimidating and there's a good chance the police will stop you and ask what you're doing. Of course, this does give rise to some interesting conversations.

"We're doing spiritual mapping," you reply.

"Of course you are," they say.

But by this time you should have developed a good relationship with your local beat bobby, and you should have let him know that you want to go round and pray. He should have informed the Duty Sergeant and there shouldn't be a problem. (At worst, he'll know you're harmless; at best, he'll be glad to see you.)

Walk around the town quite normally; you'll appear to be chatting but you'll be praying as well. Put your footprints on the street, have a look around and see what's going on, and pray all the time for wisdom and discernment. I've talked about your prayer supporters: you need people interceding for you when you're out on the street. Take maps and make sure you get to know the area, and do that prayer walk.

Talk to people along the way, and don't be ashamed to explain what you're doing if they ask. Talk to the local shopkeepers and go into the pub and chat to the licensees. Let them know you're out there. They may think you're a bit weird – people have thought that about me all my life, but it doesn't bother me and it shouldn't bother you. Don't be put off: "The one who is in you is greater than the one who is in the world" (1 John 4:4 NIV).

Prophetic acts

When I was a young Christian I was working on a tough London estate, and we went on a prayer walk. We got some pretty strange looks – the place was well known for the massive problems it had with drugs and alcohol and violence. One of the pastors showed us a house where drug dealing went on, where people could go in and drink and watch porn films.

We went out several nights in the week, praying around the area and meeting people. We even talked to some of the guys going in and out of the house. Then one night a man came along with a bucket of water.

"What are you going to do with that?" I asked him. "Wash the car? Or wash your hair?"

"No, I'm washing the street," he said, and threw the water along the pavement. "It's a prophetic act, to show how God's Holy Spirit is going to clean up this place."

I was a bit embarrassed, to be honest. I had no understanding of spiritual warfare (and in any case, I thought he'd said "a pathetic act"!). But I certainly understood the results: the drug den closed down, the people moved out of the house, and the street began to come alive. Kids started playing football in the street again, because their parents were no longer afraid of what they might see or what they might get drawn into.

We serve a mighty God.

6. Appoint a team leader

You may be the manager or the project leader, or whatever title you choose, but you can't do everything. You need a team leader who can inspire and lead the rest of the team.

This person needs to be someone who totally owns the vision. Together you need to sit down and talk through all the stages in the project, and consider your volunteers. The team leader's job is to discern who has the right gifts for work in the different areas. If someone is sporty, they can probably get a football team going (or basketball or skateboarding – whatever's popular in the area). If someone has the gift of prayer, get them to visit your local churches and explain what you're planning, and then ask for and lead prayer.

There are so many other tasks, and the team leader should be able to find the best people for them all: drivers are vital to drive the bus (if you have one) or just pick up and drop off teams at locations; accountants or other people good with figures need to look at the budgets and work out what the costs will be. You may have gathered a good team, but the leader is the one who co-ordinates it all and gets it up and running.

You should have a job description for your team leader, but you'll recognize the right person: they're the one who has come alongside you, who is inspired by what is happening and wants to see the vision go forward.

There is one danger: sometimes you come across people who seem to be keen, but who want to change that vision completely – either to fit their own dreams and ideals, or in response to minor setbacks or events. Don't allow them to hijack the project. God has given you this vision, and adapting it to develop something similar on someone else's terms won't work. It sounds inflexible, but you shouldn't compromise: if God has given you the vision, God will give you the right people.

The other thing to be aware of is succession planning. You may not be spending the rest of your life running this project, and maybe neither will your team leader. Make sure you always have your eyes open for the person who will take over from you, and start training them early. Your aim is not to be indispensable, but to be an enabler, so that the project can go on running in the future.

7. Train and equip your volunteers

Training is vital for several reasons. If your volunteers are properly trained, you can wave certificates at official bodies, and that makes them take you a lot more seriously. And people who have had the right training have more confidence in themselves and their ability to do a job. If your kitchen staff have been trained in hygiene and food handling, if your teams have learned how to handle aggressive behaviour, and how to deal with child protection issues, they will stand a little taller, respect their own abilities more, and trust their own authority – and that rubs off on the young people. And if your team are volunteers, giving up their time for free, it's only fair that you invest in them, for the long-term good of the project. It's the professional thing to do, and it's important.

One of your first tasks is to get training for yourself – in team management. Seek it out; often volunteer bureaux will be able to give you good advice. This will help you to avoid unexpected pitfalls and give you the confidence you need to deal with your volunteers and the various problems that can arise when any group of people are working together. Topics you might explore are deciding what roles you need to fill; what policies and procedures you will need to enable people to work effectively; how to decide on job specifications; how to recruit your volunteers; how to screen volunteers; how to train them; how to supervise them; and how to give feedback and motivate them. If you are going to issue any kind of contracts, you will need help in framing them so you know exactly what you have signed up for.

The next task is to train your team, and you will need to decide what this will involve. These are big issues, and a good way of tackling them is to get your team together in a relaxed setting. Go out for a coffee and a sandwich, or go bowling, and get to know each other. Then sit down and work out the training needed to achieve your goals.

It's a good idea to ask your local agencies to help you: lots of local community groups will let you join in with their training. There may be a small cost, but you should include this in your budget, because it's so important. I did the secular training for youth and community workers, and it has been invaluable.

First aid

There's a whole range of skills you need. For instance, first aid training: you can go to St John Ambulance or your local college for a course. It won't be expensive but it will give you the basic knowledge for dealing with an emergency on the street. We're not talking about open-heart surgery here, just the basic checks on breathing and airways, how to put someone in the recovery position, how to stop bleeding and so on. I keep up my training and do a refresher course every so often. Of course I'll pray for someone who's unconscious, but I'll also do the practical things necessary to help someone stay alive. Think about the Good Samaritan:

he wasn't commended for praying for the man who got mugged, but for binding up his wounds and getting him to a place of safety.

It's good to pray for wisdom and spiritual discernment, but don't forget good old common sense! You'll encounter many different situations on the street, and eight out of ten times these problems are drink- or drug-related. You need to know what to do. In any group of twenty people, I'd recommend that at least four are trained first-aiders.

Handling aggression

One of the most important skills you need is knowing how to handle aggressive behaviour. By that I don't mean knowing kung fu or karate. It's incredibly dangerous if you have a hefty volunteer trying to defuse a potentially violent situation by saying, "Let me through, I've done martial arts." Then you *know* it's all going to kick off.

What you need is to understand the basics of body language, how to recognize aggressive behaviour, and how to talk to people who are getting agitated. Alcohol reduces people's inhibitions, and drunks can get very angry very quickly; whether a situation gets violent can depend on how you deal with them.

This is another situation where it's vital to have both male and female volunteers on your team. You can get into difficult situations very fast if a male team member tries to restrain a female who is causing trouble on your bus or at your club. You need males to deal with males and females to deal with females, and they need to be trained. As Christians, violence generally plays no part in our lives – but on occasions it may have to. There are times when you need to forcibly restrain a young person to prevent them from assaulting another, and this is not only acceptable but necessary. However, the law does not permit the use of disproportionate force. Training will help you know how to use force effectively to keep yourself and others safe.

Drug awareness

One thing you will need to keep up to date is your knowledge of drugs. You need to know what is available on the street and what are the up-and-coming drugs. There are always new drugs out there, and you need to know what they look like, how they're used, and what their effects are. You may find tablets or liquids, or even be shown them. Different drugs become fashionable in different areas, and you need to know what the latest craze is so that you're aware of what's going on when you're on the street. Your team needs to be equipped with this knowledge. When young people tell them things, they need to know when it should be kept as a confidential request for prayer, when something has to be reported by law (such as sexual or violent abuse), and when they should call the police or an ambulance (when someone has taken a particularly harmful drug or alcohol combination).

The police are very good at delivering drug awareness training, but there may be other organizations in your area which can provide it (see www.talktofrank.com).

8. Know your aims

An essential part of training your volunteers is ensuring that they understand your aims – and you may need to complete other parts of your outreach strategy (area assessment, spiritual mapping etc.) before you make a final decision about the exact details of your project, which is when you can develop your aims and objectives. It's no good just saying, "It's a Christian project which will go out on the street to reach young people." You need to be more specific: What do you hope to achieve? How are you going to get there from here?

You will need to draw up a constitution which includes these aims, and make sure that they are owned and understood by the whole team, not just the organizing committee. (See 'Setting up a constitution' in Chapter 1.) Then, when anyone asks any of the team, "What are you doing?" they'll all be able to answer (and all the answers will be much the same!).

You need to decide whether your aim is long-term (to go into an area for two or three years and put a strategy in place for the long haul) or short-term (to set up a festival or information centre for a weekend). Are you going into the park in the evenings just to talk to young people and befriend them? Or are you planning to provide information about alcohol, drugs or sexual health, with the aim of enabling young people to make informed choices for themselves? (That's important, because you can't do it for them.)

All this is important for several reasons: armed with a secure knowledge of your aims and objectives, you can give presentations to churches and secure prayer support; you can ensure that your team understand your wider purpose and the methods you will use to achieve it; and you can convince councils, the police and other agencies of your professionalism.

These are the questions which will come up at council meetings, because the bodies which grant you permission to park or offer you funding will want to know what you will be doing. Of course, if your project works well, everyone will see the fruits of your efforts, but you must know what your objectives are before you start. Apart from anything else, you can't evaluate a project's success if you don't know what you were aiming to achieve.

9. Pray for the finance

Yes, the money comes *last*!

This is the big one. Most people think that praying for the finance for their project comes first, but it doesn't. I know of well-planned projects where people have been praying for a long time, then suddenly someone comes along and says, "God has put this on my heart; I'll give this amount of money to the project", and you know that the prayer has been answered.

The money comes last for a reason. If you keep badgering people for money before you've done any detailed planning, they will be understandably wary of committing to your project. They won't want to put their hard-earned cash into your pocket until they know what you're planning to do with it. It looks like a big black hole for finance – you can keep dropping money into it, but will anything ever come out of it? Who knows?

Whereas if you have detailed plans, they can assess for themselves what the need is, and how likely you are to be able to fulfil your promises. They want to see that you know what you're doing, that you'll be accountable, that you'll have auditors checking your accounts, that the money will be spent wisely – then you can pray the money in.

There are lots of ways of getting funding. It's great if you can persuade local businesses to make contributions or maybe underwrite the whole project. You're more likely to get lots of smaller contributors – local people or churches who agree to invest in the project, perhaps paying for specific items like fuel or food, the tuck shop, or the running costs (people often like to know exactly what their money is going to). Wise stewardship with money is very important.

It's good to pray for funding – God will often tell one of his listening servants that this is what he wants them to commit to. But you shouldn't let this be the be-all and end-all, and get hung up about the money side of things. God will provide the money when you have put your vision into action though planning and training.

A letter from the police

In 2001 we held a lot of events in the Manchester area, including a "Make a Difference" scheme, where a large number of agencies came together with the local community to clear rubbish and remove graffiti, and renovated two areas to be used as community resources in the long term. The Eden buses were important to the overall success of this initiative, attracting large numbers of young people and engaging them in positive activities. Whenever the Eden bus was there, reported incidents fell in that location, and the police began to take a close interest in what we were doing. This resulted in a commitment on the part of the local police authority to make a funding contribution. An Inspector in the Greater Manchester Police wrote:

Since your involvement just once a week we've been able to have some feedback from the young people and their parents, which has been very positive indeed. One or two youths are still problematic and cause a level of concern, but given the level of deprivation and social problems being experienced in this area this was only to be expected. The local youths still flock to you and your team each week, which speaks volumes. The number of reported incidents while you are there still reduces significantly, which highlights how well your team engages with the youth. The reason the project has triumphed is directly down to the dedication, patience, understanding and leadership that you have displayed, which I know not only inspires your team members but gives youths the confidence to return each week.

It is not only my intention to continue the partnership, subject to funding which I know is not your main consideration, but I would like to explore the possibility of extending and expanding your involvement into different areas of Manchester which are also experiencing similar problems. I believe you and your team are contributing to the long-term solution in the area and will continue to do so. I am delighted that we have been working with the Eden bus team and look forward to a long and successful partnership.

Chapter 6

Working Together

There may be some amazing preachers and evangelists who work entirely alone – though even they generally need a back-up team, whether it's administration to set up their speaking schedule or just someone who makes their sandwiches! But I think it's safe to say that most outreach work relies on teamwork. You need other Christians to work with you at every level – from the other churches in your community, through the many volunteers who join your project, to the smaller number of individuals who work on your team on any particular day. Jesus sent out his disciples in twos – surely teamwork is what he wants from us.

Working with local churches

Local churches are the resource which enables your ministry. They can be a source of:

- prayer support
- information
- volunteers
- finance.

Seek them out, listen to their advice, share your vision with them, and ask for their prayerful support. Make a presentation or have an open evening, and provide refreshments and an opportunity for worship and prayer. Make it as lively as you can: use DVDs, PowerPoint and real people. Interview some of the young people you've been working with, and get them to talk about the project and what it does. It will give your audience a taste of the conditions they'll be working in, and also an idea of how much the work means to people in the community. Have flyers ready to hand out, with a list of your aims and objectives, so everything is absolutely clear.

Your project may represent a particular denomination, but try not to be insular about this. There will be other churches who know what's going on in the area, and who have their own set of relationships and local links. Add their knowledge and skills to your own, and you've got a better chance of success: we're all on the same side, and Christian unity is a powerful tool. Christians who share your heart for their local community will be generous with their time and money, no matter what denomination they're from.

They also provide the nurturing environment for young disciples. Outreach work, by its very nature, goes out of the church and onto the street – but people who have found faith need to move on, into a worshipping community of other Christians, so that they can grow. If you have established relationships with local churches, you can feed people into the church environments that are suitable for them. Tastes differ – one person likes a church where they shout from the rooftops, another prefers a quiet, meditative service; some people like jazz bands, others like a choir. Link yourselves with a variety of churches embracing different styles, and you have choices to offer your new Christians. Young people in particular like places where they see other people of their own age, and where an effort is made to do things at their level.

Working ecumenically is a great strength – you can do so much more than a single church. Christianity's main focus is faith-based, not denominational. When I was a new Christian I thought "ecumenical" sounded like a new brand of washing powder – I had no idea of the differences between churches, and I didn't much care. I still don't: when people ask me what denomination I am, I say I'm a Presbyterian Baptist monk! In other words, I'm just a Christian and particular brands don't come into it. Denominations are like roast beef: some people like it well done, others like it medium or rare. It doesn't matter what style of worship you prefer, as long as Jesus is at the centre.

One of the challenges non-Christians most often throw at us goes along the lines of: "Look how many denominations there are. If you Christians can't even get on with one another and agree, how can you have anything to offer the rest of us?" There is strength in working together, if only to prove how little those differences matter to us. You may have to overcome your own prejudices a bit, and remember to focus on what you share with other churches – your faith in Christ – and not what differences of practice divide you. If you have several churches on board with a project, it creates an awesome witness: everyone can see the churches working together for the local community, with God at the helm.

Working with volunteers

Every project depends on the volunteers who staff it: your task is to recruit them, get to know them, assess their skills and manage them effectively, as well as invest in their future. It's a big job.

Recruiting

One of your most challenging tasks will be to recruit people and assess their gifts. Some will be able to take on what you ask of them immediately; others will need to grow into their roles; but occasionally it's important to take a risk. We've all been there, learning on the job and finding our way. Provided they are receptive to training, they will probably emerge as excellent team members. You can give them the opportunity to blossom.

Remember to cast your net wide: try advertising in youth-work magazines and *Christianity* magazine as well as locally. Put posters up in your local churches – volunteers from the local community are always valuable. Take from a range of age groups: gap-year students will have time available, as may some of the over-sixties. We only used over-eighteens (because of legal requirements) and I felt I had to cap the age range at eighty-six! We had one man in his eighties on the bus, and he was tremendous. He told stories of the war, the hardships of rationing, and living on bread and dripping, and the kids listened in amazement. He had incredible faith, and the young people really respected him.

You should also be prepared to take on others who offer, including people with disabilities and learning difficulties. They may need a little extra support from the team, but they will be able to communicate with people who have similar disadvantages. Always ask people what their vision is – you'll soon be able to tell if they are happy to share in what you're trying to do.

Don't be afraid to bring in people from outside your area, maybe from the suburbs into your inner-city location (or vice versa). They can bring different qualities and experiences to enhance your team. Sometimes you will be able to arrange for students (or others) to move in with a local Christian family for six months or so; they may be supported by their local church with finance and prayer. Outsiders may find it easier to think outside the box, and see potential which the locals (and you) have ignored, because you're too close to the problems to see the way through.

At the same time, value your locals, because you can't beat having people on board who live and/or work in the area and know its history.

Watch out for the inexperienced!

Some volunteers need a bit of supervision and help before they reach their full potential – but it's worth taking a risk on them, even if you occasionally have to step in and retrieve a situation.

I knew that Simon was a lovely young man: he was a keen Christian from a solid Christian family. He lived in a "nice" part of town, but he had a real heart for the kids living on the deprived estates in the inner city, a passionate faith in Jesus and a vision for helping other people. Unfortunately he was seriously lacking in the wisdom needed to communicate with kids on the street.

We had given him a chance to speak in the God Slot, and he stood up and told them that if they took drugs they would go to hell. You can imagine how well that went down. People started swearing at him: "Who are you to tell us what to do?" He was losing control of the session and the kids were getting really angry. I took a step forward and put a hand on his shoulder.

"What Simon's trying to say is that drugs are really bad for you," I said. "They take you to a bad place. Turning your life around can save you from all that." I managed to rescue the situation without making him look silly (and stopped them from attacking him!).

Afterwards we sat down and discussed what went wrong. Simon was mortified. "But people will go to hell," he said. He was really upset that his message hadn't been listened to. I explained to him how to give that sort of presentation, and how to make it a personal testimony ("I believe this") and not a denunciation of other people's behaviour, which isn't our job. Some of those kids knew about hell because they were already living in something that felt like hell to them. Our job was to give them a message of hope and love, not of condemnation.

I wanted Simon to grow, and he did. We had some of our people work alongside him, and eventually he became one of our best speakers.

Interviewing

It seems silly to turn people away when you're desperate for volunteers, but the fact remains that some people just won't be suitable. How do you find out? By interviewing them. This need not be as intimidating as it sounds. Remember that you are recruiting volunteers, not employees – your job is to make them feel valued, whether you accept them onto your project or not. You may be able to tactfully redirect them into other activities.

You need a panel of at least three interviewers, both male and female. For the panel you need people who think clearly and are disciplined – it's easy for interviews to go off track. They also need to understand your vision and know something about youth, community and family issues. A Christian policeman or social worker would be good, and magistrates are also trained to ask relevant questions (without making people feel as if they're in court!). You need people who understand the issues and who can pick up on people's motivation and their strengths and weaknesses.

It's also important to notice what questions the volunteer asks you. This may indicate how well they understand what you're trying to do. Show that you appreciate their enthusiasm, but challenge them: ask what unique qualities they can bring to your project. If they just say they want to evangelize, try to encourage them to go a little deeper – how do they see themselves doing that? Why do they want to get involved? I once interviewed a girl who had offered to work with us. When I asked questions, she said that she wanted to do some work... and meet people... and eventually admitted that she really hoped to find a boyfriend while working on the project! We didn't take her on, because she was just too vulnerable.

You should also keep your eyes open for potential leaders, the people who can be trained and mentored until they're ready to take on leadership roles.

A job for everyone

We need to explain to people that whatever they're prepared to do – cleaning the toilets, stocking the bar, driving the bus, staying at home and praying – there's a job for them, and they too can be part of the big picture. There are people who care about the project but don't want to go out and work on the street: they may be able to help by emailing newsletters, designing flyers or writing press releases. We had people who used to make a big pot of soup and bring it along for the young people and the volunteers to share. Others collected clothes and blankets for the young people who were homeless. Even if they can only give an hour a week, they can pick up volunteers and drop them off at the work location, or phone some friends and have a prayer session.

CRB checks

The whole issue of Criminal Records Bureau checks is undergoing some changes (including changes of name) at the time of writing – there are hopes that soon all the information will be held centrally. Meanwhile, the best advice is to check out the current situation by going to the website (www.crb.gov.uk). What will not change is that anyone wishing to be involved with youth work will need "enhanced disclosure" – this is a list of all unspent and spent convictions and cautions held on the Police National Computer and local police systems, together with any relevant non-conviction data held by the police (such as where an allegation has been made but not proceeded with). In most cases this will simply be proof that a search for such information has been made, and nothing found.

All this information is strictly private and confidential (so it's important that you and any others involved understand the need for confidentiality). It provides a clear indication that your volunteers have been cleared to work with children and vulnerable adults. This is vital for your project, so the cost of getting it should be borne by the church or organization, not the volunteer. When the check is being done for paid employment, the disclosure document goes directly to the employer, who can open it and read it, and then pass it on to the employee. When it's for a voluntary post, the document goes first to the individual, and they can produce it when asked by the organizers of the project.

This is not just a matter of boring bureaucracy – it's really important. I get exasperated when church members say, "But we have to trust each other" or "We'll be all right if we just pray about it." You must do these things properly in the eyes of the law and according to best practice in the secular world, if you want to be taken seriously.

In any case, it's not about condemning people for what they may or may not have done in their past – you'll be more willing to trust them if they are prepared to be open about any past convictions. You will be able to ask them how things have been going since their drink-driving ban, or their Class C drugs offence. These are not necessarily a reason to exclude people from your project. My own CRB disclosure reads like a book – I had a string of early convictions from the age of sixteen, including a spell in prison. I'm not proud of it, but they were all petty crimes, not relevant to working with young people. In fact, some of these past offenders can be among your most effective workers. It's very impressive when someone is willing to stand up and say, "I messed up in the past, but now I've got my life right with God."

However, if someone refuses to show you their CRB check, don't take them on. I once had a man who said, "I don't want to show you my disclosure form – but I promise you there's nothing on there about child abuse or anything like that." It turned out that he had convictions for domestic violence. He would not have been suitable.

Of course, CRB checks are not fail-safe; they only pick up the people who have already been caught. And most of the people you take on will be worthy of your trust, and you won't have a problem. But the important thing is that the CRB check covers your back. If anything should happen, and you hadn't gone through the CRB process, the press would have a field day and you would quite justifiably be criticized for not taking an elementary precaution to ensure the safety of the young people in your care.

Mentoring

Sometimes your volunteers will come from within the project itself, among the young people you're working with. I've had kids come up and say, "I'd love to do what you guys are doing." My response is usually, "Why not? What are you interested in? If it's youth work, let's sit down and explore the possibilities."

Of course, we're a Christian organization, so I would want to see them settled in a Christian fellowship for at least a year first. This will test their Christian commitment and provide some accountability. Then we give them a mentor from the project. The young person can go with them as a silent partner, watching how they do things; they can be involved but not hands-on, learning and observing. The mentor can get to know them, find out their strengths and weaknesses and train them accordingly. Often they can be incredibly effective, because they're working on their home patch, so they know all about the drink, drug, crime and other problems, the deals going down and the people who need help. A young person from your target community who has been trained and mentored will be a key part of your work. And when you and the project eventually move on, they will still be there as a witness. It's an important part of the vision that you should have that kind of voice in the community.

The mentor has to tread carefully, both accepting the young person as they are, and at the same time encouraging them to live the kind of Christian life that sets an example. No one changes overnight, and the Christian life is a process of growth. You have to consider how plausible it is for them to carry on hanging out with their friends while working alongside you on your project. There needs to be a certain level of dissociation from their old life, if what you stand for is to be believed.

Changing a life

Dave was a young guy who became a Christian on the Eden bus, and we were very excited for him. He had a lot of baggage – including problems with drugs and alcohol – but we could see him maturing and growing.

However, he couldn't quite tear himself away from the peer pressure of his friends. He was ready to stand up and say that he had become a Christian, but he thought he could still stand outside the bus having a smoke, and he could still get drunk with his friends in the pub. The local people saw him as a bit of a joke: he didn't appear to be any different from the way he was before he became a Christian. In fact we knew he was moving on with God, but he was still pulled by his old life.

Eventually we got him onto a discipleship training course which ironed out some of his issues. He stopped going out drinking with his friends. He still had a battle with smoking, but he didn't smoke around the bus or with his friends. He really wanted Christ to be Lord of his life, and he began to work at it. He understood that he couldn't expect people to take his testimony seriously if he was showing no signs of faith in his daily life.

Working with your team

No matter how well researched, well funded and well staffed it is, every project depends on the day-to-day teamwork of the people on the front line: the volunteers in the bar, on the street, or in the bus tonight. It's essential that you develop the skills and establish the good practices that enable the best teamwork.

Your basic role is to be a pastor to your team. You will be overseeing the work of volunteers who are giving up their time and energy to support your project, without any payment. They must really want to do it, or they wouldn't be there. Of course they trust that God is watching over them, but they also need to trust you. They need to know that you, as team leader, are watching their backs; that you have put everything in place so that it's safe to do the work they're involved in; and that you'll communicate with them. If there's no trust in the team manager, the project will ultimately collapse, as people do their own thing and then everything falls apart.

Communication

Communication is vital – a project is no place for Lone Rangers who go off and do what they want without telling anyone. Never assume that volunteers know what you're thinking: always double check that the message is clear and that it has got through. I've heard people say so many times, "I just assumed they'd know…" Sometimes it's a basic safety matter; sometimes it's that a visit has been cancelled for what seem to you to be obvious reasons. Always check. Nothing is more demoralizing for people than turning up for an event that doesn't happen, or finding something has happened and they weren't there.

Prayer

The team that prays together… You know the rest. It's important to the project to set it up with prayer, and it's even more important to the individual teams that each session's work is prepared with prayer. Get the mechanics right, and make sure you make space for it.

Don't meet for prayer on the estate where you'll be working, or in the building if it's a club or bar. You'll only be interrupted. Go somewhere you won't be observed, and where you can hold a briefing meeting and prayer session in private. It's useful to have half an hour or an hour set aside for this: it can be an opportunity to recap on recent events and make sure everyone's up to speed before you start work, as well as committing the evening, the young people and your own work to God. You can pray for protection, for wisdom and discernment, and that God will do amazing things in that session.

Attendance at prayer time provides a good assessment of people's priorities. The leader has a life and responsibilities of his own, and it is just as much a sacrifice of his time as everyone else's. If your volunteers always turn up late for the prayer time, or even miss it entirely, you should challenge them – what is more important than prayer here? You don't need to be judgmental, but they can often relate to your own responsibility and see how they are letting everyone down. Some people are just a bit slapdash; they turn up for the last five minutes, because all they really want to do is get on with the work. Then they're surprised when it all goes wrong.

Sometimes it's a simple matter of missing out on information. If you've warned the team that "Johnny lost his uncle today, so he's upset, and he's likely to kick off," they can bring it in prayer before the Lord, and they're also forewarned. If some team members weren't there for that, they won't be prepared.

Prayer is the backbone of what we're doing. At the end of the evening, we need a debrief on what happened, any information about the kids and their lives, or how the team have felt about the evening, and take all that to God in prayer too.

Sharing jobs

However you have organized your evening, whether it's on a bus, in a bar or in a club, don't stick people in one job for the whole time. Just because someone is good at being on the door, don't leave them there, because they won't get the chance to grow into the other work. In any case, the big guy who looks intimidating isn't necessarily the best doorman: a little old lady may be quite firm and forceful and no one will lift a finger to her! Working on the door all evening can be quite demoralizing, if all you deal with is the guys who have been drinking and have to be turned away, while the people who really want to take part and engage with what's going on disappear inside. After half an hour of being sworn at and having things thrown at you, you might want to throw something back!

Instead, you should aim to swap jobs every half hour or so. A fresh face will have a fresh approach, and the previous doorman can sit down and have a drink, and get a chance to talk to some of the young people. That way you stay sharp, which is especially important if you're doing outreach work in a volatile area. Sharing jobs keeps the team alert, watching one another's backs, and it ensures that they're all aware of which young people are there that evening, and they all know which kids are edgy and likely to cause trouble. Remember that people can grow and develop. It's OK if they really love one particular task – let them fly with it – but only once they've had the opportunity to try out some of the other jobs on offer.

Being aware

One of the key skills when you're working with large numbers of young people is being aware of what's going on around you. You should always know where your team-mates are; you need to be constantly making eye-contact with the others. We have always used a lot of unobtrusive sign-language between us. For instance, I might look at a colleague, point to my own eyes and then to a youth; no one else notices but the volunteer knows who they should keep an eye on. Occasionally, if I see someone having a conversation which seems to be getting out of hand, I might make a motion with my hand across my throat to indicate, "Cut it off, you're aggravating them."

Other people's awareness is especially important if you have to handle any kind of discipline – telling someone they have to leave the bus, or intervening if kids are getting violent. You should always make sure that team members are around, keeping you in earshot and in view – then, if it all kicks off, they can move in swiftly. We also used to have CCTV cameras on the bus, in case of disputes, so that we had filmed evidence that we had never used unnecessary physical force. This is where job-rotation comes into its own, because everyone has worked all around the room or bus, so they're all aware of the various scenarios going on that night. It's a bit like being at the theatre – you watch what's going on, but you never know what's going to happen next. There's so often something simmering away in the background – relationship problems, rival gangs or personal problems. If you pick up on it all early, you can put a strategy in place for dealing with it.

Tough streets

It's not just the young people you have to watch out for – sometimes you have to calm down your own volunteers.

One night I was working on the bus with a new team member called Jim. A gang of lads from outside the area came along and started bricking cars parked in the street, some of which belonged to our volunteers. Jim was furious and wanted to go over and challenge them, and I had to hold him back. I told him to stay on the bus and cool down: "Thank goodness it's just a car getting damaged, and not your head." One of the bricks went right through a car radiator, it was thrown so hard. We gathered all the kids on the bus and shut the doors for safety: if a brick could do so much damage to a car, what would it do to a child?

Later on Jim realized that this kind of thing was part of the job we had taken on, and accepted it. The guys didn't know anything about the Eden bus project, they just wanted to cause a bit of trouble. Getting us to chase after them was exactly what they wanted. Later on we had another incident where young men were driving round in cars, firing guns in the air. It was very dangerous but we couldn't pack up and go because we had forty young people in our care. Once again we shut the doors and got them to keep low for safety.

This was something our volunteers had to accept as part of what they had signed up for: sharing the reality of life on some very tough streets.

Keeping in touch

Working effectively with your team means keeping in touch, even if you're out on different streets. We found out early on that mobile phones – even older models – are desirable and saleable objects, and they will get stolen. Walkie-talkies are much more useful: they're not cool, a single one is no use, and they only work on restricted wavelengths. It's vital that your outreach workers have a means of communicating with you, especially if they're in any kind of dubious situation. When a group of kids hanging around in a dark park hear the distinctive sound of a walkie-talkie handset, they know you're in contact, you might even be the police, and that in itself may be enough to calm things down. We found it was very rare for a disturbance or fight to involve our team, but it was good to know that if it did, they could call for back-up.

Working the streets needs detailed planning, and you need to use a map and mark on it where you will be. Your outreach teams in that situation should be no more than four to six people (more than that, and you have what starts to look very like a gang), and you must set a working zone and agree that no one will go outside it. Then, if you should need to go in and help, you know where the team will be – near the chip shop, or by the pond in the middle of the park – and no one should be out of touch.

Never go into "dead" zones where the walkie-talkies don't work. It's no good saying afterwards, "We were concerned about you," if something has kicked off and the team was left with no support.

These are worst-case scenarios. Most of the time there's no trouble, and all these precautions aren't necessary. But like any insurance system, if the time comes when you need them, that's when you *really* need them, and you'll be glad you had them in place.

Being in control

Your team is your major asset – none of the work with young people could go on without them. And communication is vital at every level, because you are accountable for your team when you're out there. Yes, God is in charge – but he has put you there to take care of the detail, and it's your job to protect them. Doing that may mean being firm with the team members themselves, because a wayward volunteer who won't accept instructions and wants to do his own thing can cause a lot of trouble.

Occasionally you get team members who say, "I'm just going over there – it's OK, I know those people," even if where they're going is outside the agreed zone. It sounds such a little thing, but it can cause huge problems. You don't have to be a dictator, and with luck you'll be able to make your point with humour and understanding, but you have to make it clear that the team has to stay with the agreed strategy. Some of the places you'll be working in are genuinely dangerous, with guns and knives in the hands of people whose judgment may be impaired by drink or drugs. A place that looked safe a minute ago can rapidly turn into a riot zone. And someone who thinks they always know best can put the whole team and even the project in danger.

If you find you have team members who really refuse to follow instructions and believe they know better, you may have to ask them to step down from their role. Everyone's safety depends on everyone working together.

The maverick

Alex was a volunteer with an outreach team who were working on the streets of a tough estate. He was a valued member of the team, but had broken the boundaries set down by his team leader several times, and he always laughed it off. He thought we were making too much fuss – he could handle himself.

One night he was talking to a gang member who admitted that he was scared of walking home, and Alex decided he was going to go with him, even though the lad's house was outside the safe zone for the outreach team that evening. They went off alone, without telling the rest of the team where they were going.

As soon as they reached the other side of the estate, a rival gang attacked them, and Alex was quite badly beaten up. He managed to contact the rest of the team and call for help, and they called the police and came to get him.

We had to ask Alex to step down from the team for six months: he could have got a lot of people injured. If he had told someone else, the team could have assessed the situation and found another way round it – perhaps even driving the bus slowly alongside the lad to escort him home. As it was, Alex had shown that he couldn't act responsibly, and he insisted on acting alone. We couldn't guarantee his reliability and therefore his safety.

Chapter 7

Being Professional

Suppose you are a parent, and your kids come home asking to join a Saturday craft club. There are two on offer: one has a well-produced flyer, printed on good-quality paper. It says the name of the club and the church organization that runs it, together with the place and the time of the meetings. It says what its aims are ("To show children the love of God in action while being creative and having fun") and how it plans to achieve them ("Run Saturday-morning craft sessions in a safe, fun environment"). It says that it operates a child protection policy approved by the local council, and that all its volunteers are CRB checked. It says that a qualified first aider will be on duty at every session. It gives full contact details for a named leader, and its Charity Commission registration number.

The other club has handed out a photocopied sheet of A4 paper bearing the name of the club, the place and the time.

Which would you be more likely to send your children to?

We need to operate in a professional manner because we want people to trust us. However, getting people to come along to our events isn't the only reason to be professional.

Gaining credibility

Our main reason is that we are working for God, and so we want to be the best that we can be. That means observing the current best-practice guidelines for whatever we are doing. However, an important secondary reason is that we need to gain credibility with the relevant secular agencies. We will need to liaise with them for support, training, and organizational and legal requirements (for instance, you may need permission from the local council and/or the police if you want to park a bus on the street).

Other agencies

You may find you want to liaise with:

- Police
- Social Services
- Probation Service
- Youth Offending Service
- Individual schools and colleges
- Local Education Authority
- Town Council
- District Council
- Youth and community agencies
- Local churches.

Before councils and other agencies will take you seriously and agree to work alongside you, they will need to see that you have in place a clear constitution, aims and objectives, a proper management structure and accountability, and good training. These are the key words that always come up in conversation when people are trying to find out whether you are a professional organization or not.

The aims and objectives are important because everyone involved needs to understand what they are trying to achieve. When I was working on the Eden bus, David Cameron and William Hague came on board to see what we did. (We were on BBC's News 24 – the cameraman had great fun taking shots of the street signs, which was when we realized that we had parked on Blair Street!) David Cameron asked me, "Why are you doing this?" I didn't have to waffle vaguely about how I felt about things; I was able to quote straight from The Message's aims and objectives, which were unashamedly Christian: that every young person in Manchester should see and hear the gospel message of hope and restoration. To elaborate on this I gave him a copy of my first book, *Nobody's Child*, which described how I ended up doing youth work in Manchester.

The other volunteers told him how the local crime rates fell when the bus went onto an estate, and explained that ours was a practical initiative designed to meet young people where they were. The politicians were impressed, especially when they asked the young people on the bus for their feedback, and they said how much they liked having proper youth facilities coming to them.

Even when people aren't interested in Christianity, the faith side of things doesn't seem to worry them at all, provided they can see that you're doing a good, professional job. The Celebrities Guild is a secular organization, but they gave me their "Unsung Heroes Award" because they admired the work we were doing. The police weren't at all bothered about our primary aim of sharing the gospel, but they gave several police awards to The Message because of the effect our work had on local communities. When that happens, you know you're doing something right, because people respect your work.

To gain that respect, it's a good idea to go to as many council, police, youth and community public meetings as possible. The other agencies will see that you are taking an interest in the public life of the local community (and they're less likely to see you as religious nutters doing your own thing). They will recognize you as professional people who are willing to work co-operatively and make the effort to engage with other agencies. You will also benefit from becoming a familiar face, and you will learn who does what locally, and how to approach them – it's so much easier to ask for help when you know people's names and have met them before.

Management structure

This isn't something that only belongs in big organizations or the commercial world. Line management runs from the volunteers, through the team leaders, to the manager of the project and on up to the director of the charity or the minister of the church you are representing. All volunteers should have a written job description, so they know exactly what you expect of them, and this should give a clear outline of their role, together with the name of the person they're accountable to. Everyone should have their own copy.

This means that if they should be unhappy about anything, they know immediately who to ask for help or advice: usually the team leader in the first instance, and then the project manager if necessary. They in their turn have the names of those who are responsible for them.

Everyone involved in the project should wear a badge showing their name, the project name, and a telephone number. Then if a member of the public has a complaint, or maybe just wants to check that they are who they say they are, they can ring that number and speak to the next person up the management chain. You should make sure that everyone wears their badge at all times when they're working, so that people know who they have seen and spoken to, whether on the street or in a meeting.

Training

We've already said how important it is to make sure that everyone is properly trained. You may be able to ask for training from secular agencies who offer it to outside organizations, sometimes while they are training their own staff. Sharing in this way need not compromise your message, but it can build bridges with people and groups who might otherwise regard faith as an alien concept (and its practitioners as religious maniacs – it's up to you to prove them wrong).

Some of the topics you might look for training on include:

- Fund-raising sources and techniques
- Human resources (diversity, discrimination, recruitment and managing volunteers)
- Finance (accounting, managing money and auditing)
- Communication (managing the media, writing reports)
- IT (computers and software)
- Law (charity law, legal issues relevant to your work, data protection)
- Health and safety (including food hygiene)
- First aid
- Driving (minibus/bus driving)
- Child protection.

You can get advice from the Directory of Social Change, an excellent source of information and training for the voluntary and community sectors (see www.dsc.org.uk). There are also local advice centres for the voluntary sector (like www.voluntarysectortraining.org.uk which provides services to the county of Essex) all around the country. Find out where the equivalents are in your area.

Child protection

You should get child protection training for all new volunteers, and update it every six months or so, checking out any new government policies and regulations. All churches should have a child protection policy in place, so you should be able to tap into their training. There should be someone in every team who co-ordinates child protection issues, so that if anyone discloses a relevant issue, like abuse or self-harm, your volunteers know who to tell in the first instance.

All work involving children and young people must be supervised by someone familiar with the child protection policy and who takes it seriously. This isn't just about abuse or neglect: it will also cover basic things like health and safety rules, and the appropriate number of adults to number of children (which varies according to age groups and activities).

You need to have your own rules, too: we said that there should be no adult on the bus (other than our own staff and volunteers) unless they were the parent or guardian of one of the children. We had to say this because we were there primarily to provide a service for young people, but other people sometimes wanted to come and see what was going on, and on a cold night the bus looked a very attractive place to hang out. It could even be that some of them were drawn to places where there were lots of children.

We had three people on the door at all times: we called them the Guardian Angels and the Grappler. The Guardian Angels were smiling and welcoming; the Grappler was there in the background to be the restrainer in case of need. He was trained to be able to bring someone to the floor safely and with the minimum of force. When you have a sixteen-stone drunk coming along at 9.30 p.m. and trying to barge past the slightly built Guardian Angels – that's when you need a Grappler.

What would you do?

One evening we parked the bus on an estate and a young mum came along with a baby about eight or nine months old. Everyone thought he was really sweet, and some of the girls gathered round cooing over him. The baby was sitting in front of a computer screen, fascinated by the pretty colours and dribbling away, when we suddenly realized that the mum had decided we'd make a handy baby-sitting service and left him while she went off to the pub!

We realized that we'd been "had". We didn't know where she'd gone, or even if she'd actually abandoned the baby. We had to leave some people to keep an eye on him while others went off to try to find the mum. We had a real problem, as the end of the session was approaching. We couldn't drive off and leave the baby in his buggy on the street, but we couldn't safely leave him with anyone else. If we had called the police or Social Services the whole estate would have been up in arms against us for "shopping" her – and we couldn't prove where she had gone.

Fortunately a member of the same family was upstairs – but we couldn't just hand the child over to him, either, unless he could prove he was a family member. We were just trying to work all this out when the mum turned up again, quite oblivious to all the fuss. She'd only gone off for a quick drink, she said; what was our problem?

When you draw up your policy you can get advice on what documentation you need, but in general it should include a statement on the following lines:

> The Newtown Youth Project is committed to safeguarding the welfare of children and young people. It recognizes its responsibility to take all reasonable steps to promote safe practice and to protect children from harm, abuse and exploitation.
>
> Paid staff and volunteers will endeavour to work together to encourage the development of an ethos which embraces diversity and respects the rights of children, young people and adults. The Newtown Youth Project will:
>
> - ensure that all workers understand their legal and moral obligations to protect children and young people from harm, abuse and exploitation;

- develop best practice in relation to the recruitment of all workers;
- ensure that all workers understand their responsibility to work to the standards and procedures detailed in the project's child protection procedures;
- ensure that all workers understand their obligations to report care or protection concerns about a child/young person, or a worker's conduct towards a child/young person, to the project's designated person for child protection;
- ensure that all procedures relating to the conduct of workers are implemented in a consistent and equitable manner;
- ensure that the designated person understands his/her responsibility to refer any child protection concerns to the statutory child protection agencies;
- provide opportunities for all workers to develop their skills and knowledge particularly in relation to the care and protection of children and young people;
- ensure that children and young people are enabled to express their ideas and views on a wide range of issues;
- ensure that parents/carers are encouraged to be involved in the work of the organization and, when requested, have access to all guidelines and procedures;
- endeavour to keep up to date with national developments relating to the care and protection of children and young people.

You should also have a fuller document covering your child protection procedures. This should include:

- An introduction. This should cover the purpose of the procedures; the people concerned; the duty of care; a commitment to children's rights; the names of the individuals responsible for setting up and reviewing the policies.
- Recruitment. This covers the necessity of CRB checks.
- Summary of types of abuse (physical injury, neglect, sexual and emotional abuse) and how volunteers should look out for them.

- Procedures for responding to concerns that a child is suffering abuse inside or outside the project.
- Summary of the referral process, when it is appropriate to discuss the concerns raised, and reassurance for volunteers who report concerns.
- Data protection and management of confidential information.

When you obtain training in child protection you will get advice on how to prepare and update these documents.

Risk assessment

Risk assessment involves taking a careful look at your project, the premises, and the activities you get involved in, weighing up what could go wrong, and working out what you can do to prevent accidents happening. It's important to protect everyone involved in your project, as well as to comply with the law if you are employing anyone. It helps you to focus on what could cause harm to anyone, and gives you a structure for doing checks and taking steps to make things safe. Some things are straightforward (like cleaning up spills promptly, or fixing loose carpet) and others are more complex (like working out what could go wrong in an activity and making sure people know what to do).

You can't possibly eliminate all risks, but the law does require you to protect people on your premises *as far as is reasonably practicable*.

Whatever your project – whether it's in a church, a mobile unit or other premises – it's better to get someone outside the organization to do the checking. You know your own environment because you're familiar with it, but an outsider sees it with fresh eyes. Getting Public Liability Insurance requires extensive checks, and you need to make sure these have been done as thoroughly as possible. Someone should survey the premises and make an initial assessment, then make recommendations for improvements; you must follow these or you would be liable if any accident happened.

The simplest method is to follow the five steps advised by the Health and Safety Executive:

- Identify the hazards.
- Decide who might be harmed and how.
- Evaluate the risks and decide on precautions.
- Record your findings and implement them.
- Review your assessment and update if necessary.

See www.hse.gov.uk for more advice.

You need to think laterally: what *could* happen? Suppose you take a group to the park to play football: is the pitch uneven? Could someone twist an ankle? Are there syringes lying around? When you park your bus on the street, could the kids run out onto a busy road when they get off? If you have a generator room, are the petrol cans locked up? Do you have emergency lighting if the generator fails? Do you have an emergency plan for when that happens (as soon as the lights go out, kids start screaming and everything kicks off; if you have fluorescent strips on the floor at least everyone can find their way to the door). Do you know what you'll do to disperse people if the crowd round your bus gets too big or too wild?

In Appendix 2 you'll find a template for risk assessment, with some examples.

CCTV

CCTV is a luxury that most projects can't afford, but if the finance is available, cameras can give everyone additional protection in case of trouble. Sadly, allegations can be made against youth workers and volunteers by angry young people, and it's very reassuring for everyone to know that everything that goes on is caught on camera.

The Eden buses had cameras on both decks with access to all points of view. They were protected with wire mesh (so they couldn't be smashed or pulled off the wall), and the workings were hidden in a locked office (so that no one could grab the tape or disk and run off with it). We also had a camera with a microphone fixed to the rear of the bus. It was useful for safe reversing on a very long vehicle — but it was also amazing how often we heard young people out there laying their plans to set fire to the bus or to let the tyres down. They were always shocked when we said calmly, "Well, guys, before we can drive off, you'll need to remove the bottles from under the wheels."

We always asked respectfully that people should remove caps and hoodies, so that their faces could be seen when they were on the bus. We had to put up a sign saying that people were being filmed for security reasons. No one ever complained. We never had a toilet on the bus because it would be an unsupervised area where people could get up to mischief, and obviously we couldn't have a camera in there.

Candid camera

There was one night when we had a lad who was causing trouble and hit a younger boy, so we asked him to leave the bus. He went quietly enough, but just then a police car happened to come by, patrolling the area, and he waved it down. He told the officer that the bus driver had assaulted him, dragging him off the bus and punching him. A policewoman came over to investigate, and I knew that if she had to record it as an incident, it could be very serious; the project's reputation was at stake.

"I understand," I said. "But before you talk to the volunteer in question, do you mind if I have a chat with this young man, in your presence?"

She agreed, and I turned to the lad. "OK, I appreciate what you're saying," I said. "One of my team members will get into serious trouble if you continue with this allegation. You're entitled to do that. But I just want you to know that we've got the whole evening on video, so everything that's happened anywhere on the bus tonight is caught on camera and can be used as evidence. If you want to change your story, now would be a good time."

The boy looked over his shoulder and saw the CCTV camera. He swore and ran off – he knew nothing had really happened, and the film would show him being asked to leave and getting off the bus on his own. Without that vital piece of equipment it could have been a very different situation.

The images of people that you collect are covered by the Data Protection Act 1998 (as is information about them, such as car registration numbers). Most CCTV use is covered by the Act, no matter how many or few cameras you use or how simple the equipment is. The government has issued guidance to help organizations who use CCTV to do so responsibly, called *The CCTV Code of Practice 2008*. It is an updated version of the original code of practice, providing advice on how to comply with the Data Protection Act, and a checklist for users of very limited systems where the full provisions of the Code would be too detailed. See www.ico. gov.uk or contact the Information Commissioner's Office at the address shown at the back of the book.

First aid

It may seem obvious that you need to have someone trained in first aid on your team. The danger is that people get very excited if there's an accident or event where someone requires help. For every volunteer who panics at the sight of blood, there's another who thinks he can do open-heart surgery because he watches a lot of *Casualty*. He'll be stripping off someone's shirt and thumping their chest at every opportunity. And it's always the attractive girls who faint and get offered the kiss of life!

The problems come when people try to remember their Boy-Scout training, which is usually out of date and lost in the depths of their memory anyway. All you need is enough knowledge to assess the situation accurately, to check airways if someone is unconscious, to call an ambulance if necessary and to keep the person warm and calm, to make sure they are not given any food or drink, and to get contact details from them if you can.

Keep an incident book and write down the date and time of the event, the name of the person involved, and any treatment which is given (even if it's only a sticking plaster).

You can get training in first aid very easily. The Red Cross provides training geared specifically to the workplace (see www.redcross.org.uk). The St John Ambulance (www.sja.org.uk) provides not only courses for the workplace, but also courses for the general public, and for young people and for those who work with them. Their combined "Emergency and Basic First Aid" course covers first aid, how to deal with minor conditions and those that become more serious, and how to resuscitate a casualty. It lasts six hours and costs £40 at the time of writing; the certificate is valid for three years.

Finance and accounting

Money is the one of the biggest causes of the failure of projects – not the lack of it, necessarily, but bad management of it. Attacks on and criticisms of Christian ministries most often have their roots in financial irregularities. No one expects you to be an accountant, but there has to be a fundamental awareness among the team that the public have put their hard-earned money into your project, and whether it's £1 or £1,000, it has to be accounted for.

Who holds the purse-strings in your organization? As a manager, you are responsible to the auditors for how the money is spent. You always need at least two signatures on cheques, as a safeguard (the bank will give you all the details when you open the account, but you should get some proper accountancy advice before doing so). Your job is to make sure that every penny appears in the accounts. That means telling all your volunteers that they can claim expenses (for sandwiches, petrol or anything else you have previously agreed), but that no money will be paid out unless they can produce a receipt. You must keep all the receipts safely, because the auditors will pick up on any missing documentation; without receipts, there's no evidence that the money hasn't gone straight into your pocket.

If people give money for a specific part of the project, it has to be ring-fenced, and it can't go into the all-purpose funding pot. So if someone makes a donation towards the fuel costs of the bus, you can't spend that money on wages. If you did so, and the auditors discovered it, you could lose your charitable status.

All charities must prepare annual accounts and all registered charities must prepare a trustees' annual report. The Charity Commission (www.charity-commission.gov.uk) can give you lots of advice about this. They publish guidance notes on charity reports and accounts, including templates for the layout and content of these, as well as information about opting for independent examination instead of an audit. Look for their *Receipts and Payments Accounts Pack (CC16)* and their *Accruals Template Packs (CC17)*.

Chapter 8

Handling Aggression

Throughout this book I have mentioned that when you are working with young people in some circumstances, you will encounter aggressive behaviour. This may not be the first thing some people think of when they plan to take part in youth work, but it's a fact of modern life.

Difficult behaviour is not confined to the "sink" estates and deprived areas: you can get it in the leafy suburbs among youths from middle-class homes. Nor is it confined to boys. In May 2008 Richard Ford wrote in *The Times*: "Figures from the Youth Justice Board showed that crimes carried out by girls aged between 10 and 17 years old have risen by 25 per cent in three years, with violent attacks against people rising by 50 per cent."

Although some people blamed the trend on the "ladette" culture and underage drinking, others said that the statistics reflected the fact that criminality by young girls is taken more seriously than in the past.

There's no doubt that alcohol plays a large part in violent behaviour, and it's also the case that nowadays the police become involved in situations that once would have been dealt with in homes or schools. But there are other causes. When the *BBC News Magazine* reported the same figures under the headline "Why are girls fighting like boys?" one reader commented: "It's quite telling that of the three images used in your article, two are from the soap *EastEnders*. Makes you wonder how many youths see this kind of fighting on TV and just assume this is the norm."

If we want to manage difficult kids, we need to look more deeply for the causes which lie behind their aggressive behaviour.

Why are they so difficult?

There are many reasons for antisocial behaviour, and it pays to get to know the young people you're working with, so you will develop some awareness of their lives.

Lack of childhood

It's easy for churches to miss this problem, because Christians who are trying to structure their lives on biblical principles tend to regard family life and nurturing their children as priorities. The degree of neglect which some children suffer is almost unimaginable to Christians.

I have seen seven- and eight-year-olds told to get out of the house, and walking the streets with a baby brother or sister in a pram. Our girls used to play with their dollies, but these children have a real baby to look after. They often have to cook their own food because their parents have passed out on the sofa after drinking or taking drugs, or they go into their mum's purse for some money to buy chips. The police have told me that it's usual to see quite small children in the street at ten and eleven o'clock at night, hanging round the kebab van in the hope of getting something to eat.

I once met a family in the street together, and asked the father for permission to take a photo of their little boy. He was six years old, and he had a can of beer and a cigarette. The dad was quite happy for me to take the picture – he thought it was perfectly normal. Is the church ready to cope with a six-year-old in Sunday School who has to go outside for a cigarette?

A professional response

I met Sandra hanging around outside the bus in Manchester. She was only eight or nine, and you had to be eleven or over to get on the bus, so we couldn't let her on. She looked so lonely that I hopped off and chatted to her. It was a hot summer evening but she was bundled up in a heavy winter coat.

I was clowning around a bit, and did a handstand on the pavement.

"Go on," I said, "if I can do it, you can."

She shook her head. "I can't do that. I can't go upside down – I've got nothing on."

Her mum had sold all Sandra's clothes for a few pounds to buy drugs.

I never liked going to Social Services, because I always worried about the possible backlash from resentful families, but I knew I would have to report neglect of that nature. When Sandra had gone home, I went round the back of the bus in tears. You think you've seen everything and then one little girl's life really breaks your heart. My gut instinct was to give her a hug and tell her that someone cared for her, and I badly wanted to promise to bring her some of my girls' clothes, but I knew that I had to be objective. The professional response was to chat to Sandra (she only wanted some company) and then to contact Social Services.

In fact there was a good outcome from that evening. Her mum did have some idea of what she was doing to her little girl, and was ready to get help for her drug problem. I hope Sandra's life improved.

Many parents seem to forget that their children are just children. I especially notice how many little girls are dressed in sexy clothing – even seven- and eight-year-olds. You could say that this is just the society we're living in; after all, that clothing is on general sale in ordinary shops. It may be a danger-point for society that we are sexualizing young children, but what does it do to the children themselves? They attract attention, but for all the wrong reasons. What will they regard as normal behaviour? Once or twice I've mentioned to parents that I think their children's clothing isn't appropriate, and they've generally had a go at me: they think I'm just an interfering "do-gooder", and it's their business what they choose to dress them in.

Rejection

Young people have an enormous need for love and acceptance, and their self-esteem suffers if they feel rejected at home. Older children may feel pushed out when the focus is on younger siblings or a new baby, and they often start behaving badly just to get noticed. If their parents have their own problems – exhaustion from working long hours, or the worry of unemployment or debt, or the difficulties caused by drug or alcohol abuse – the children's needs are likely to go unnoticed.

Sadly, it may be the same kids who feel rejected at school. Perhaps they have learning difficulties which haven't been recognized, or which they have covered up by bad behaviour, so they are stigmatized or excluded. The result is more loneliness – if the home is dysfunctional and school is closed to them, where will they find friends? When they're seen as rebellious, the chances are that they will attract others in the same situation, and gangs of excluded kids are the most likely to drift into antisocial behaviour and crime. Even there, it's easy for an individual to be rejected by their peer group for the most trivial reasons, maybe because they don't have the ideal body shape, or because they have no money or status.

They seldom appear to be lost or lonely: they get used to covering up their hurt feelings, and pushing all emotion down out of sight. Aggressive attitudes and rebellion against authority are a coping mechanism, as they assert themselves in an effort to feel more important.

When they come into contact with a Christian organization, and you start talking about God, you are likely to come up against a whole host of unspoken assumptions. One, sadly, is that God as Father may not be a good image; the concept of a loving father may be completely outside their experience. They may never have thought about God before, but once you start telling them about him, they immediately assume that he will reject them, too.

This is sometimes a real issue for the children of Christian families. When the parents are busy "on God's work" they sometimes give the impression that they don't have time for their own children, who feel understandably resentful. God has an optimum order of priorities for us: God first, family next, work last (even if it's working for the church).

That doesn't mean we don't work hard, but we make sure our family doesn't always come last. Unfortunately some people seem to put things in a different order: work, then God, then family. Some high-powered businessmen, youth workers, pastors and vicars may see less of their family than the manual worker or the unemployed parent who makes time to be with them. It is a hard fact to face sometimes, but I am one of those parents who has benefitted from taking a look at my work schedule and family life and making some adjustments.

Emotional needs

When parents don't know how to express affection (often because they, in their turn, were poorly parented), the children's emotional needs remain unmet. When there are no hugs or reassurance to be had at home, the kids will seek emotional support elsewhere. This may mean joining a gang or being available for no-strings-attached sex, which they mistake for affection.

In 2009 the Office for National Statistics reported that underage pregnancy rates had increased: 22 under-16s became pregnant each day in 2007 (the latest year for which figures are available), a total of 8,200 girls. On the BBC's Today programme Hilary Pannack, of the sex education charity Straight Talking, said, "We are failing a whole generation of young people... We really have to tackle the underlying causes of high teenage pregnancy rates. It is to do with self-esteem and self-respect."

Family situations

When children have grown up in a situation where the parents use alcohol and drugs, where abusive language or domestic violence is the norm, they copy what they see. It's not surprising that they exhibit similar behaviour when they turn up at your youth project.

Often they are growing up with poor (or no) parental supervision; one or more parents or siblings may be involved in crime; their living conditions may be unstable (with frequent moves between properties or into bed-and-breakfast accommodation), and there may be physical or mental health issues. Some families are accustomed to a string of interventions by the school, the local authority, the police or Social

Services, trying to address the effects of family disruption, truanting, child abuse, neglect, crime or imprisonment.

Economic disadvantage

Some young people develop a strong sense of resentment because of their economic circumstances: they see other kids who have "stuff" – clothes, designer labels, the latest phones, iPods and so on – which they covet. We may well disapprove of such materialistic priorities (we probably get along very happily without many of those things), but it's a consumer world in which they live, and it matters to them, especially where status among their peers is related to possessions. It doesn't have to be logical: it's still a factor in why they exhibit anger.

There are more profound effects of poverty and deprivation. Debt and money worries are not confined to parents: often their children are well aware of the threat of eviction or of the bailiffs knocking at the door, and this can affect their mental health. Poor diet can have long-lasting effects on people's physical health and well-being, and even their day-to-day energy levels. Kids who haven't eaten properly can be lethargic and lack concentration, and then get high on the sugar and caffeine in a can of Pepsi. Meals on wheels are still delivered to the elderly, but I often wish they were available for teenagers. Too many of them are given a pound to get some chips for their dinner, and the idea of getting five pieces of fruit or veg a day is a joke. Their estate will certainly have a chip shop and a pub, but probably nothing more. If the government really wanted to do something about their health, putting a cheap greengrocer on every estate would be a start.

Bullying

We've all seen the headlines: children committing suicide because of bullying. Schools may have anti-bullying policies, but even where they are successful, the bullying can shift to the virtual world where people are ridiculed on Facebook and Bebo.

We would like to think that our youth clubs are the safest place for young people to be, but we are naïve if we think that bullying doesn't happen there, too. We tend to deal with the loudest and most troublesome teens, who are competing for our attention, and lose sight of what may be happening to the quiet ones.

A child who has been bullied once will expect to be bullied again: low expectations lead to low self-esteem. The kids who are overweight, or not quick-witted or confident enough to answer back, or who have hygiene problems, will be picked on at school, and even if they come to your youth project they will probably expect to be bullied there, too.

Helping at home

Sheena was a single-parent mum with two teenage girls. Our church made contact with them because they went away for the weekend and left their dogs in the house alone. The barking disturbed the neighbours who called the RSPCA, who broke in to rescue the animals. What they found horrified them: the place was filthy. The toilet had got blocked and the family had been using the bath instead; there was animal excrement on the carpets and there were wild rats as well as tame ones running around.

The animals were taken away, and when the family came back Sheena was furious. However, one Christian went round and befriended her, and realized that most of her anger was due to a sense of shame. She hadn't dared to ask for help because she was afraid the council would evict them, but she hadn't had the energy to tackle the problems.

The house was cleaned up and the girls were delighted; they hated the squalor but didn't know how to deal with it. The filth and the lack of washing facilities meant that they smelt bad themselves, so they got bullied at school, which made their low self-esteem worse.

Once the family had been shown how to get the place clean, they managed to keep it that way. The church community worker made regular visits, so if the toilet blocked or the shower stopped working, it could be fixed. And the girls started coming along to the youth group and making friends for the first time.

Fear

Many young people live in a permanent state of fear. Some worry about passing exams, about their parents splitting up, about finances at home, about friendships, relationships, or even world issues. Some live with serious fears: one parent may come back from the pub drunk again, and they don't know when their parents will start hitting each other or even the kids. If drugs are being sold on their street, they're not sure about going out because the dealer may be cruising round with a gun in the glove compartment of his car. If they step over the unseen boundary into another gang's territory, someone may come after them with a knife. They feel they have to watch their own back, because no one else is looking out for them. And their nervousness spills over into aggressive behaviour and bullying, because if they look tough, maybe no one will risk facing up to them, and they'll be safer.

Common indicators

All these factors can lead to insecurity and anger, which in turn are manifested in various kinds of antisocial behaviour. Young people who are full of repressed emotions will take out their feelings on anyone. They are especially likely to react if they sense disapproval, which touches on their lack of self-worth. This means that they may respond abusively or violently to anyone they recognize as representing authority: teachers, vicars, youth workers, police, paramedics, firemen and so on.

The Centre for Social Justice published an interim report in 2006 which recognized that debt, economic dependency, failed education, drugs and alcohol addiction were all massive contributors to family breakdown, and all were implicated in antisocial behaviour and criminality. The same patterns of social deprivation are linked to patterns of youth crime, and this held true in research all over the world, from the USA to Europe, and from Australia to Asia.

Volunteers working with difficult young people should be aware of this. It's important that we don't reject anyone (however bad their behaviour), but try to understand why they act the way they do.

Setting boundaries

Many of these problem kids will never have had any boundaries; no one has ever cared enough to be bothered about what they do. We all know that teenagers in homes where boundaries have been set will always push against them, testing them. Does Mum really care what time I come home at night? Does Dad mean it when he says my music mustn't be too loud? If I break the rules agreed on at home, will there be repercussions? At a time when they're finding out about themselves and the world, firm boundaries give them security.

Teenagers will rebel against "rules", especially when they have been set by other people. "Boundaries", however, sound less like rules imposed by an arbitrary authority, and more like limits put in place for safety reasons. They are like a notice placed at the cliff edge, warning of danger. Boundaries don't have to be broken, because they can be a bit elastic; they're there for a reason, but they can be stretched to accommodate different situations. In some scenarios we can negotiate exactly where the boundary needs to be.

For example, one of our boundaries was that no drink was allowed on the bus, and young people who had been drinking were not allowed on, either. Then one evening an eighteen-year-old came up with a can of beer in his hand, and wanted to come on. I told him he couldn't bring alcohol on the bus, and he said he would either finish it or put it in the bin.

Should we have let him on? It's not illegal for him to drink at his age, and he certainly wasn't drunk – I believed him when he said the half can was all he had consumed – and he was being sensible and polite. On the other hand, if another young person smelt the alcohol on his breath, it might look as if we were allowing drinkers.

In the end we let him on (without his can), and he behaved perfectly well, and no one complained. We had to make an informed decision on the spot, and be seen to be fair. It would have been different if he had been underage or affected by drink, but it seemed like a sensible time to stretch that particular boundary.

The problem with this sort of flexibility is when the volunteers on the door are intimidated by a six-foot-tall lad and let him on the bus, even though he has been drinking, and then exclude the small guy or girl, just because they're easier to deal with. That kind of thing breeds anger because it's seen to be unjust.

The way we managed it was to sit the young people down when we were starting up the project and ask them what they thought. That came as a surprise to them – they weren't used to being consulted. Once we got past the silly suggestions, they made some sensible ones: no drink, smoking or drugs. They could all see the sense in those rules.

It's OK to be firm. Once the boundaries have been agreed, it's important that you stick by them and remind the young people that they have helped set them up. There's no reason why you should have to put up with bad behaviour or insults just because you're a Christian. Too often we're seen as soft targets, and that's because sometimes we're afraid to stand up and say what we believe and why we believe it. We should insist that everyone is valuable in the sight of God, and because of that, everyone is entitled to respect and safety. I often say to young people, "I may be a Christian but I'm not a muppet." There is such a thing as righteous anger; the kids know that I'll stand firm, for the sake of the project, and that gets their respect.

Dealing with difficult behaviour

Prayer is the backbone of what we do, and this is especially true when we know we'll have to deal with difficult and disruptive young people. We need to pray for patience, understanding, grace, wisdom and discernment, and for protection for the whole team. Then we move on to specific people (either on the team or among the families we meet) who need our prayer support. Everything we say about dealing with aggressive behaviour must be seen in this light: our ultimate guide and protector is God, but he has given us common sense and the ability to learn, and he expects us to use every human tool at our disposal in dealing with people in a safe, friendly and professional manner.

What isn't acceptable?

Drink and drugs should have absolutely no place in your project: none may be brought onto the premises, and anyone thought to be under their influence should be excluded. Smoking can be a tricky topic: it's easier now that there's a universal ban on smoking in public indoor spaces, but lots of people are so seriously addicted that they really can't face a whole evening indoors without a cigarette. So you'll always get a group of young people hanging around outside smoking. What happens when your team members are also smokers? What they do in their own time is obviously up to them, but they can't go out and smoke alongside the young people while they're working, or there's no difference between them and the youngsters – and it means they have left their post.

Swearing isn't acceptable, either, though you will sometimes have to point out which words are swear-words. Lots of young people are used to hearing swearing all the time, every day, and they barely register the words, so it's a good idea not to make this one a hanging offence. They often don't realize how offensive it is. The way you react to it will affect their response, and provided you don't act shocked or horrified, they will learn to moderate their language over time. Any deliberate verbal abuse must, of course, be dealt with.

"Play-fighting" can be another potential problem. Young men, particularly, are always delivering playful punches and pushes to each other, but horseplay can develop rapidly – especially if someone gets hurt rather more than was intended, and hits back. Before you know it everything is kicking off, and it's much harder to stop it than to prevent it starting. You'll have to keep a watchful eye and make sure you calm things down.

If you are trying to keep order, backchat makes it much harder. You know the scene: you spot a young person lounging on a chair with his feet on the table, so you ask him to move them, and he responds with a joke, or "Who's going to make me?", or swears and tells you to leave him alone. How many times are you going to ask him? We always used a traffic-light system to give them three chances. The first time, you ask them to stop doing whatever it is, giving a reason ("Please take your shoes off the table – you've been walking in the street and you could have dog poo on them"). The second time, you deliver a warning ("If you keep doing that, you'll have to leave"). If you ask a third time and they refuse, then you put the warning into action and they have to go. It sounds harsh, but it stops things escalating and it makes the point that someone is in control of what goes on (and it's not them). It means that the young people know that there's a cut-off point, that you won't get involved in arguments, and that there are consequences to their choices.

Physical control

Some Christians feel very strongly about avoiding violence, and say they would never use physical force against another person. However, there are occasions when it's necessary. Forcibly restraining a young person from hitting another is not violating their rights, it's protecting someone else. I have also had to restrain someone under the influence of drugs for his own safety, because he was repeatedly banging his head against a window.

Some volunteers understand the issue of defending themselves or other kids, but think they can use their own abilities (like kick-boxing) freely. If they are expert in martial arts, their arms and legs can be used like weapons, and indiscriminate use of force on their part can make a situation escalate wildly. You need to know that while restraint is OK, the law does not permit you to use *unnecessary* force to restrain someone: it must be proportionate.

Drunk and disorderly

One night we had a run-in with a boy who was very drunk. He was only fifteen, but he was a big lad, tall and broad and weighing about sixteen stone. At first he wasn't aggressive at all, telling us that he loved us and we were the best, and trying to persuade us to let him on the bus. "You've got more chance of being prime minister than of getting on here," I told him, which he thought was very funny. He walked off, laughing, then suddenly turned and ran back towards us – he had gone from being "silly drunk" to aggressive, in the blink of an eye.

As usual, we had four people on the door, two welcomers and two heavyweights. He barged into the first two, knocking them over and forcing his way into the entrance, trying to attack us. The next two managed to get him down on the floor and restrain him. The whole team was on high alert now, and all our safety protocols were in place: we sat all the young people down and kept them occupied and away from the action at the front; we had our walkie-talkies operating on earpieces, so we could talk privately; the driver had the police phone number at hand at the press of a button, and he started the engine so we could pull away if we needed to.

Everything seemed to be going all right for a while, as the team had succeeded in restraining the boy without harm to himself or others. Our welcomers talked to him (they always worked in a mixed team, because women seem to have a calming effect on aggressive young men) and got him back on his feet. He agreed to leave – but then jumped off the top step of the bus onto the grass verge. He landed awkwardly and twisted his ankle, so we had to call an ambulance and his parents. Because he didn't want to tell his parents that he had knocked two people down, he said the team had assaulted him, so the paramedics called the police as well.

Once again we were saved by the CCTV record: he finally admitted that he was showing off when he jumped, and that he fell down because he was drunk.

Some situations are trickier than others: how does a man restrain a young girl who's kicking off and trying to punch everyone around her? First, you always stand sideways-on to her: it's safer (because she can't easily get a direct hit out sideways) and less confrontational. You can put your hip sideways against hers and get a hand round her shoulders or waist, or under her arm and up to her shoulder. These positions ensure that there's no inappropriate contact – you have to be careful that you're never in a position which could be sexual in any way. You should also always have a female colleague on the other side of her – and you will have other colleagues watching, and preferably our old friend the CCTV. Never restrain a female (however strong or violent) with two male volunteers.

Managing aggressive behaviour is never about strength or weakness, but about teamwork, staying calm, and refusing to be provoked into anger. Understand your own body language as well as the young people's: take a relaxed and non-aggressive stance, make eye-contact with the person concerned, and maintain a friendly, confident manner. That alone can calm people down. But you should always be on the alert for someone who is getting out of control, so that you can prevent the situation from getting any worse. Make sure you get some training for the team in safe methods of restraint, and practise the moves in role-play so you know where you should be: a drunk won't realize that you are unobtrusively positioning yourself ready to restrain him if necessary. Your job is to protect the other young people and protect yourselves, and it's surprising how rapidly you can resolve things if you're well prepared.

Debriefing

At the end of the evening, don't let the team just drift away, no matter how tired you are and how much you just want to get home. It's important to close the evening with prayer, and to check up and resolve anything that people may be unhappy about.

This is the moment to raise any issues, before they get forgotten. While you are working, it's vital that you support the team 100 per cent – even if they do something wrong – but you should address the mistake later on. For instance, if someone is banned from the project (for swearing or fighting, perhaps), it's important that you don't make an exception: it compromises the whole disciplinary set-up. No individual has the power to change decisions that have been made. But if someone does just that, and lets in someone who has been banned, you must just go along with it during the evening. You should never reverse their decision or criticize a colleague in front of the young people. They will quickly pick up on any differences and exploit them. Instead, make a mental note to raise the issue in the debrief.

If there has been violence, you should make an opportunity for people to talk about it. No matter how "hard" some people like to think they are, physical violence and verbal abuse can be shocking, and they need the opportunity to let their feelings out and deal with them. There may be tears or laughter. It's not enough to say, "That was awful – let's pray about it." Ask the team how they feel about it now, how they felt at the time and how they coped with the events, and let them off-load their anger or anxiety, and learn from each other.

I once got a black eye while restraining a young man. I wasn't too bothered (apart from having to explain it all the time), but it had a tremendous effect on the family. It was harder for the girls to believe me when I told them that Daddy was quite safe when he went out at night, and even Gillian was more than usually anxious about me. I had to take some time out and consider their feelings as well as my own.

Chapter 9

Don't Switch Off!

The final part of any Christian youth work session – no matter how crazy the activities have been – is always the God Slot, and this is the bit that frightens people the most. They may be willing to go into the toughest streets, befriend the most difficult young people, or do the dirtiest and most menial jobs because they love their Lord and want to serve him. But ask them to talk about Jesus – or even to make space for someone else to do so – and they get cold feet. "They'll just switch off," they say. "They don't want to hear about faith."

The important thing is that what we are doing is never "just" youth work. It has to have that added dimension of faith, or we will fail in our aim, which is to give young people the opportunity to know Jesus.

A good youth project has the potential for being very successful. I know that young people have a great time when they get on the buses run by The Message. I could set up a good business running fun buses, and make thousands of pounds by charging people £1 a time to get on. But that's not the purpose of what I do. As a Christian, I want to inspire young people, and empower them to make informed decisions about their lives. I want to see them grow and develop through the life-changing experiences of faith that we can offer them. It's a privilege to share in God's purpose, and tell them about his love.

I've been to visit loads of youth clubs which are very popular: they have brilliant volunteers working there, they have fantastic activities and use all sorts of technology, visual aids, puppetry – all the media for effective teaching – but there's no mention of God. Nearly always the leaders say they're afraid the young people won't be interested, that they'll switch off and get bored if they start talking about religion. Some say, "We don't do a God Slot, but the young people know we're Christians." My answer is, "How?" If you don't mention the fundamental reason why you're doing the work, how are people to understand anything about your faith? It's not enough just to be there – that *is* "just" youth work.

I've had years of experience in youth, community and children's work, and every project I've been involved with has had a God Slot. I've never compromised on this, and over and over again I've seen young people's lives dramatically transformed by God working in them.

The God Slot

You can give it a cheesy name, put some sort of spin on it, anything you like, but ultimately the God Slot is what it is – a bit of time set aside to make space for God. It can be an opportunity to share personal testimony, to read the Bible, a time of worship, or drama, or discussion, but God is at the centre of it.

I always recommend that you make this session part of the set-up from the very start: you're more likely to succeed with it because there won't be any hidden agendas. If you get your project under way, and then suddenly try to introduce a God Slot halfway through, you'll have a battle on your hands: people will resent it because they'll feel they've been conned.

Like everything else, it pays to have thought out the organization thoroughly before you start. It doesn't have to be long: just ten or fifteen minutes at the end of your session. Try not to have to compete with anything else – the X-Boxes or the PlayStations or dance music. You need to turn everything off and clear the decks for God. There's never any compulsion about attending, and people must always be free to choose whether to stay for the God Slot, but the option of other activities is not available. It's the end of the session, and if they don't want to join in, it's time for them to leave. We've regularly had sixty people on the bus or in a non-alcoholic bar, all staying for the God Slot.

There's no reason for people to "switch off" – provided what you offer is interesting. That means good Christian music; professional, relevant DVDs; lively talks; and up-to-date and exciting visual aids.

What's it worth?

One little talk I've given uses a £5 note. "Who wants this?" I ask, and everyone shouts or raises a hand. I tear it in half. "Anyone want it now?" I ask. "You could have £2.50 each!" They get a bit confused at this point. Then I screw it up, pop half in my mouth and chew it – who wants it now? Usually still a few hopefuls hold out a hand. I drop it on the floor and tread on it – and remark that I think I trod in some dog's muck earlier. Not many are still keen to get their hands on it.

So I straighten out the wet, dirty, crumpled bits of note. "You don't want it any more. But is it worth any less, if I take it to the bank?" They know that you can stick the bits together and the bank will still give you £5 for it. The note still has the same value.

Then I explain that even when our lives are really messed up, and we feel that no one has any use for us, we're still valuable to God.

You can lead discussions about issues that are important to the young people you're working with: sex, drugs, alcohol, divorce, death and bereavement. Don't shy away from confronting reality if someone's parent dies: we can't be counsellors but we can offer to pray for them, and kids often draw great comfort from that. If someone's mate has died in a car crash, they may well be asking, "Why did God let it happen?" We can discuss that, and whether it was God, or the choice of the driver to have that drink.

Don't pretend to have all the answers, and don't start Bible-bashing. Just be ready to talk about your own life, and share your personal experience of how you've dealt with things. I'm lucky enough to have a DVD that was made as a promotional tool for my book *Nobody's Child*. It's very powerful, and I can talk about it afterwards. I'm not ashamed to share what God has done in my life, and I've been in places as bad as you can imagine. That I'm standing in front of them with my life made whole ensures that they're willing to listen to what I have to say.

Too often young people have strange ideas about Christians, that they're all perfect, and never argue or get things wrong. You can use your team to share the stories of their personal walk with God. You're unlikely to shock the kids, but those stories give you credibility, when they realize that you've been through some of the stuff they're going through. What's valuable is that you're not telling them how to live their lives. Instead you're telling them how you live yours. If you lay down the law and get dogmatic about faith, people can disagree with you – they're entitled to their own opinions. But if you just tell your story, they can't deny your personal experience. All you're saying is, "This is how it was for me."

Watch your language

If you're a Christian it comes naturally to use scripture when you're talking about your faith. Of course you'll want to use the Bible: "God so loved the world that he sent his only Son…" What does that mean to us today? It can go one of two ways, and it depends largely on the language you use. If you use highly theological terms, the young people will shut off. Some kids might not understand words like "Trinity" or "redemption". You need to use everyday language to discuss how people respond to God. We're not using the Bible to discuss the incidence of the semicolon in the Second Book of Chronicles: we're using it to tell people the wonderful news that God loves them. That's when the truth is likely to dawn on them, and they'll be interested enough to want to hear more.

We need to get excited about what the Bible has to tell us. We can see what happens when people trust God in the toughest situations. We can read love stories in the Song of Solomon and the Psalms; we can read about the tough men of God like David and Gideon; we can read about the faithful women like Mary and Esther; and there are enough stories of sex and violence to engage anyone! If you want a hero, the Bible is full of them – and they're not super-heroes, but flawed and fallible human beings, so we can identify with them. This attitude is good for teenagers who have never heard the Bible told like this before.

Where's the Allen key?

Sometimes I show the kids a flat-pack shelf kit, and tell them about when I went to IKEA. I opened the pack but I couldn't be bothered to read the instructions; I tried to put it together but it all fell apart. It wasn't strong enough to hold anything when you put any pressure on it.

The Bible is the Maker's instructions for our lives. When we ignore them, things fall apart, and we try to blame everyone but ourselves.

We shouldn't be afraid to share our excitement. If you go to a Manchester United match, people will laugh and cry and hug each other – so we shouldn't be ashamed to share our enthusiasm for Jesus.

Our faith is part of our everyday lives, not something we put on for Sundays, and that should be reflected in all our behaviour. That's another aspect of the words we use: what is our everyday conversation like? We don't need to lower our standards of language when we're talking with the young people, just to get alongside them, but we don't have to be mealy-mouthed either. I once had some lads on the bus who were calling one another "dick-head". I stopped them and said, "Do you know what that means? It means you're calling him a 'penis-head'." They never said it again – but I think they were a bit surprised that I wasn't embarrassed to say "penis" in public! But if Christians are afraid to say "sex", who is going to teach these kids about sexuality? They're more likely to pick up their information from TV or their peers. Let's be ready to take on the real world, in everyday language, without fear.

Don't cause offence

I do encourage you to be open and unafraid when talking about your faith, but you need to be sensitive, too. We need to treat people with no beliefs with the same respect we would show to people of other faiths. The young people know that you're a Christian, and they have voted with their feet by coming along to your project, but you can't assume that everyone is where you are in the Christian faith. You personally may not drink or smoke or sleep around, but it's no good expecting them to share your values. If you indicate, by the way you speak about these things, that you disapprove of their way of life, that can be very offensive. In an earlier chapter I recounted the story of Simon, who told his audience that they would go to hell if they took drugs. One reason he was so violently anti-drugs was that he had gone through a period of drug-taking himself. He couldn't contain his feelings of horror at the dangers they were running, and he genuinely wanted to warn them. However, his approach was wrong. We want to share a message of hope, not condemnation.

In the same way, we should respect people's unbelief. It isn't necessary to challenge them or argue with them. What we can do is quietly go on demonstrating by our words and actions the positives of faith, and the love and security and inspiration it offers.

Nevertheless, there is no need to compromise our beliefs for the sake of political correctness. We don't need to water down Christianity and say that all faiths are equal, just because we may have people of other faiths in the audience. Christianity is unique: where other faiths offer to show people the way to God, Jesus says, "I am the Way"; where other prophets offer to tell the truth about God, Jesus says, "I am the Truth"; where other teachers offer to tell people how to live in order to gain eternal life, Jesus says, "I am the Life". Our God alone offers to dwell in us through the Holy Spirit and change our lives from the inside.

People of other faiths are entitled to hold their own beliefs and opinions, and you are equally entitled to yours. In fact, I have often had parents from Muslim families sending their kids to my projects, because they knew they would be safe there, and because they trusted the morality we presented. Some of them told their kids to leave before the God Slot, but we didn't mind; they had spent the evening in the company of Christians who were happily talking about their faith all evening – we didn't confine it to the end of the session. And like the many Muslim parents who send their children to church schools, they believed that it was good for their children to spend time with people who respected God.

If people see you as a Bible-bashing zealous weirdo, you'll achieve nothing. Being opinionated and forceful and not listening to other people gets you nowhere. But if they know you are gentle and polite, that you won't thrust the Bible down their throats, and that you listen and respect their point of view, and welcome people with grace and love, then you can have some great conversations.

Show, don't tell

Similarly, telling kids how to behave never works – they'll ignore you. But showing them what it's like to live a Christian life is different: they'll draw their own conclusions. If you live in the area where you're working, they'll see how you're living. If you meet them in the shopping centre when they're with their parents, they'll watch you to see if you're the same person as the one who leads the youth project. Do you talk or act any differently? If we don't walk the walk, then it *is* "just" youth work.

This isn't a question of doing "good works"; it's about relationships, about how you treat the other team members, whether you get angry under pressure, whether you get drawn into unsuitable conversations or telling risqué jokes, or gossiping. Too many leaders and volunteers working with young people think they have to ape their jokes, language or behaviour, and it doesn't work: they just lose their respect.

You don't have to pretend to be better than you are – it's OK to admit that you've had a rough day if your goldfish just died! – but you can't show people how to act if you aren't doing it (or trying to) yourself. What you are demonstrating is the contrast between the two questions in any situation: What would Jesus do? What would the world do?

Firm foundations

I sometimes demonstrate this using two cans of Coca-Cola, with their ring-pulls intact. They both look the same, but I have used a nail to punch a hole in the base of one, and drained out the liquid. I put them both on the floor, and stand on the full one: it holds my weight easily. This is like the foundation of having God in your life. The second can looks the same, but when I stand on it, it crumples and collapses: it can't take the pressure. This is like the world. It doesn't have the strength to hold you up. I illustrate it with stories of celebrities who have fame and fortune, and everything the world can offer them, but who seek comfort in drink or drugs, and who cannot sustain meaningful relationships. The world is not enough. They have less stability in their lives than the most humble, ordinary person who trusts in God.

Long-term discipleship

It's dramatic and exciting when young people give their lives to Christ – but do you view that as the end of your work, or the beginning? Do you feel that now it's time to move on and focus on the next young person who needs your guidance? Or are you concerned that you have a young Christian before you who is just at the beginning of their journey with the Lord? They have asked for forgiveness and asked Jesus into their life, and you know that God sees their heart and knows their long-term potential. Do you have any responsibility to help them to walk safely towards their destiny?

This is such an easy step to miss. I've seen dramatic rallies where thousands of people are converted, and it's like a firework display: all flash and sizzle, and then the lights go out. If there's no system of mentoring and discipleship, if there's no preparation for helping people learn how to walk in faith, many of them will fade away and just give up.

Our job is to support young Christians as well as caring for their friends who are still searching. Sometimes I've seen a young person come to faith, and when I go back six months later, they look a bit shamefaced and say, "I messed up." Maybe they've gone back to drinking or drugs, or maybe they've just seen another relationship break down. I just say, "So what? This is a new day. Let's start again."

Most of us have had similar experiences. When we start out in faith, there's a honeymoon period, when everything is great. We're full of joy and hope and the world really does look like a different place. But we are just baby Christians at this point. God wants us to grow, so after a while he takes us off the "milk", where we are feeding off the teaching and support of other people, and moves us onto solids, where we start to learn some harder lessons for ourselves. These are the testing times, when God challenges us to grow and mature. In fact, he doesn't leave us entirely alone. I know it's a bit of an old chestnut to some Christians, but I often tell young people the poem called "Footsteps": a man looks back over his life, and sees two sets of footsteps in the sand. He knows that God was walking beside him through his life. But he sees that in some of the most difficult times, there is only one set of footprints, and he cries to God, "Why, when my walk was hardest, did you desert me?" And God replies, "I didn't desert you. You can see only one set of footprints, because that was when I was carrying you."

Everyone goes through difficult times. It's constructive: usually there are certain issues and a lot of emotional pain that God wants to deal with, freeing us to serve him with open hearts. We probably all remember the people in our lives who helped us through these times, when hope seemed to evaporate, the struggle seemed too hard, the world was too tempting, and we felt like a failure. It's our job to be there for our young Christians when they encounter these challenges. God wants us to minister to them through the Holy Spirit. Changing their lives and habits is a gradual process, and they need a safe place to grow, without feeling condemned and rejected when they fail.

Mentoring is vital for young people. They need mature, sympathetic Christians to be alongside them when they are struggling (and also when things are going well). Our churches need to be resourced and equipped for this, so the young Christians can be nurtured through prayer, worship and Bible study; they need to be placed in cell groups, taken along to Christian camps like Soul Survivor, and helped to realize that they are not unusual, but part of a huge worldwide church of followers of Christ.

There is some humility involved here. If your church is not geared up for young people, are you willing to pass them on to another church to be fed and nurtured? The important thing for the church is not getting bums on seats, but caring for new Christians in the best way.

Belong, believe, behave

Make no mistake, this is a demanding task. Conversion isn't a magic wand, and longstanding habits don't change overnight. The fact that someone has accepted Christ as their Saviour doesn't mean they will suddenly become "churchy" or middle-class – which, sadly, seems to be the assumption in some congregations.

I have seen many young people walk this path, and the development always seems to be in the same order: belong, believe, behave. First they need to belong. They need to feel accepted and loved by a Christian or a group of Christians in order to hear and really understand the message of the gospel. That's when they come to believe. Once they belong and believe, they want to be part of a fellowship and feel accepted by the church (whatever form it takes locally), and then they are willing to conform to its standards of behaviour: that's when they will begin to change the way they act. The fact that for many months or years they may not "fit in" to many people's ideas of Christian behaviour is neither here nor there: God knows what he's doing in their inner life, and it takes time for that to affect their habits.

It can be challenging for the church when young people say they are believers, but have issues which mark them out in the fellowship.

Sometimes these are obvious, like drinking or smoking; sometimes they go deeper, like their expectations from relationships. Often it's the smaller things that shock people the most: bad language, inappropriate behaviour between girls and boys, or even just nipping outside for a smoke. Sitting still and quiet for twenty minutes is hard when your concentration span is about three minutes, and no one has asked you to do it since you left school.

We have to be patient. These young people aren't joining a club where there are certain ways of doing things: they're joining a family where grace, love and forgiveness are the defining qualities. Within that family there may be disagreements, but the big thing is that we love each other. When young people come to us, are we expecting to be critical, or do we welcome them in the way the prodigal son was welcomed by his father?

It's very easy for the attitudes of church members to put young people off. I know that when I first became a Christian, lots of people didn't expect me to stick with it – they knew I had come from a gang culture where violence and dishonesty were the norms. They didn't think I was ever going to be able to change, and fit into the pattern of Christian behaviour. But over time, and with the encouragement of some valued friends, I kicked the smoking, got my silly sense of humour under control (well, some of the time!), and became more reliable. If I promised to do something, I wanted to do it, well and on time: I didn't want to let Jesus down. I'm a good example – if I could do it, anyone can, so don't put people in the "too hard" basket. The Holy Spirit is a powerful teacher.

Key issues

So what are the key issues to bear in mind when we are bringing the gospel to the young people involved in our youth projects?

First, remember that sharing our faith is our primary aim. We want every young person to know how special they are to God. To do that, we need to use the gifts that God has given us, and be willing to share our personal stories to keep our testimony real. We need to be open and honest about our own struggles – people want to see the real "you" – and never to compromise over the importance of our faith to the project as a whole.

We need to keep our own faith vibrant and alive with teaching and reading the Bible and prayer: if we don't know what we believe, and don't know what we want to say, how can we convey any understanding of what God is like? We need to make sure that what we proclaim is reflected in our lives as far as we can manage, scrutinizing our own behaviour and the image we present to the world. At the same time, we need to be gentle and forgiving of other people's failings, encouraging them to persevere and never condemning their lifestyles.

We need to meet people where they are, physically and culturally as well as spiritually. This means that when we are discipling young people, we make it easy for them to understand what we're talking about, and easy for them to feel accepted and loved. Lots of churches resist change: they say, "God is the same yesterday, today and tomorrow, so why should we keep changing to meet the prevailing culture in the world?" The answer to that is that we have to be *in* the world but not *of* it, and we mustn't make coming to church such a culture shock that young people can't adjust. If we don't keep up with contemporary culture, we will lose them. We need to offer visual aids, modern music, and activities like barbecues and camps rather than jumble sales and beetle drives. The secular agencies understand this: the government is always introducing new policies and bringing in new initiatives. Maybe it's a bit too much, but at least they're trying to engage young people. If the church is offering activities that are dated and dull, the kids will think that God's like that.

I've spent many years as a youth and community worker, and it's been a privilege to be part of the lives of thousands of young people. But I can't keep giving the same old talks or doing things the same way: I have to constantly update what I do and what I know – using Facebook, blogs, television, and everything else that's part of the world of the young people I want to reach. I still love the band UB40, but it's no good banging on about them, because none of the kids have ever heard of them. It's no good thinking Eminem is a brand of sweets. I have to keep up.

We all know the parable of the talents: God wants us to use our gifts to further his kingdom. A shrewd banker or investor won't throw money away; he invests in the future wherever there will be growth. God invests in people. Is the church willing to invest in the young people it meets, or is it willing to let them slip away for lack of resources, finances or effort? Young people aren't the church of tomorrow: they're part of the church of today, and our job is to make them welcome and make sure we're at least talking the same language.

This isn't just about how we do youth work. It's a challenge to the church: why it's here, what it has to say, and how it can live the gospel and share it. We have to be prepared to face and discuss the tough issues – death, sex, love and hate. If we can't face up to those challenging realities, we'll lose our chance with the young people. We've got to be real, we've got to be honest, and we've got to be street smart.

Appendix 1

A Policeman's View

Steve Wilkinson is a serving police officer working in Manchester, where he develops and leads youth engagement strategies for the force. He is also a chaplain to the police and is ordained in the Church of England, serving as a curate in his local parish church. An expatriate Yorkshireman, his real passion is for his adopted city, and he longs to see revival, in every sense of the word, come to it.

For several years I considered myself to be the most fortunate of police officers, responsible for all the policing in the town where we lived, involved very closely with the community, local council officers and councillors, and voluntary groups all genuinely working together to make the place a pleasanter, safer place to live.

As a family we had a fabulous church right on our doorstep, great youth activities during the week, a very keen youth worker and a young curate who were both busy in our community and lively Sunday worship led by our much-loved vicar. Our children went to nice schools and had good friends close by and both my wife and I worked near home and could be home most evenings. It really was and is a great place to live.

However, there were some serious problems, right in the heart of our town, which were proving very, very hard to resolve; perhaps most difficult of these was the crime and disorder associated with teenagers, especially on evenings over the weekend.

It's difficult to know where the problems started; some would argue it was with the Victorian townsfolk who built several large ornamental parks in the middle of residential areas. Others might say that the issue was poor parenting, and I could certainly show you families where grandmother was in her early thirties and had never had time to learn how to be a good parent, let alone show her daughter how to cope. Or houses where the kids were left alone by their parents at five in the morning so that they could commute to work, right through till late evening when they got home, which meant that the elder siblings raised the younger ones and the parents really didn't know what was going on.

Another major cause could easily be identified as cheap and easy-to-obtain alcohol, with some parents happy to drop their daughter off at the park with a bottle of wine or a four-pack as they made their way out for a Friday night in town. I'm sure there were many other causes as well, including a lack of council youth clubs, poor public sports facilities, no cinema or swimming baths and the breakdown of extended families.

Almost every week we (that is, the partnership of police, local authority officers, politicians and community groups) would come up with some new attempt to reduce the impact of antisocial and offending behaviour by drunken teenagers, rampaging in and out of the local parks and housing estates, and generally causing mayhem. When I went into work each Monday and scanned through the weekend calls, it would not be unusual to have several hundred complaints about these youths, sometimes in gangs of fifty or more, always setting fire to something, breaking windows or smashing up bus shelters, leaving piles of broken glass strewn over the primary school playground or having had a drunken party in the grounds of the old people's home.

Many Friday and Saturday nights I would go on patrol with my officers and see these huge gangs of kids running in and out of the parks. Over the years, in response to pressure from residents, I think we tried everything possible to deal with the problem: flooding the area with police and community support officers, alcohol sweeps, dispersal zones, CCTV surveillance and much, much more.

I have to say that of all the problems I faced, as the officer responsible for policing our town, it was this one that broke my heart, week in and week out. I used to walk through the parks and housing estates, often with my close friend and colleague the local authority Township Manager, and pray for the area – really pray hard for some way to help the residents who suffered from the abuse these young people subjected them to, and for the kids themselves.

What I believe is sometimes missed in the discussions about how to "deal" with youth annoyance (particularly when it is the "victims" of that annoyance who are driving the debate), is the wretched experience of many of the kids involved. Please don't misunderstand me when I say this. I don't believe in criminalizing young people, but I know with absolute clarity that there is a line, and when it is crossed the only way forward is prosecution. I've been a police officer for a quarter of a century and I am certain that despite all the help and diversion offered to them, some kids will just keep on offending. For their sake and that of society as a whole, the proper response is to arrest them and put them into the criminal justice system. However, I also firmly believe that in most cases there are other things to try before this happens, and in our town we have some excellent Youth Offending Service officers, Youth Restorative Justice workers and youth workers from the authority, faith and voluntary sectors who have genuinely turned young people's lives around.

What I realized was that for many young people, their experience of this almost feral lifestyle was wretched. They themselves became very vulnerable to abuse and to becoming the victims of crime. I know from my own experience in dealing with the kids in our area that there was enormous pressure on them to drink heavily, to have sex and to experiment with drugs. For the majority the bullying in the school playground extended into the streets over the weekends, and it was absolutely routine for younger, smaller kids to be the victims of assault, robbery and intimidation.

I mention all of this not to detract from the significant problems these young people were causing by their behaviour, but to give a more complete picture of the issue, and of where I come from as a committed Christian working in a largely secular environment. My concern was, and is, not just for the people whose lives were blighted each weekend by drunken yobs, but also for the young people involved, especially for the weakest and most vulnerable of them.

Over the winter nights of 2004 and into the early part of the New Year, calls about disturbances by young people in one particular area of our town seemed to soar dramatically. Every weekend the police would try to respond to up to sixty calls a night from one area alone, and there was good intelligence that youths were travelling from all over the town to come and "party" in that local park. The result was awful: assaults, robberies, indecent assaults, arson to park buildings, huge amounts of damage in local streets and increasingly angry residents. I remember sitting in one residents' meeting where otherwise reasonable and law-abiding people were openly talking about vigilante action. The partnership of police, local authority and community came under increasing criticism for its inability to act.

At the same time as this was happening, our church began to pray regularly about the problems in the park and its surrounding area – not in a woolly, generic way, but specifically for the place, the people and the problems. Small groups from church, police and the council would meet in the park just to pray about the problem and to try and seek a solution. Then I met a Christian colleague who had had just the same problems in her area.

This colleague was responsible for the policing in a much tougher area than I was (the problems faced there were making national news on a regular basis), and yet she had found a way to make a real difference. As a result of our conversations I started to research a project she had used, run by The Message Trust in Manchester, called the "Eden Bus", and to look at the difference it had made in her area. The Eden Bus is a fully equipped, hi-tech, mobile youth centre and is a resource available to local churches who want to work with young people on the streets rather than in a church. The Message staff help to train people from churches who want to work on the bus in their area, and then they support them over a clearly defined project aimed at engaging with young people from primary and secondary school ages.

What I found was that when the Eden Bus was used, crime and disorder fell remarkably, wherever it went and whatever the situation. I talked to people who worked on the bus and heard some remarkable stories. Of course there is a whole lot more to this than is described in these few lines: funding has to be found, and volunteers recruited, trained and CRB-checked. There needs to be wide-scale support from everyone who is involved – local council, councillors, communities and churches – and a proper project plan put together, including, most importantly, an exit strategy for when the bus project finishes.

These things are worth thinking about in a bit more depth: when I first started trying to get people to work with our church to deliver youth projects, there was some significant resistance, especially from the council's other partners. This unwillingness to work with the faith community was based primarily on three things: a fear that we would be trying to "convert" young people all the time, against their wishes or those of their families; that somehow the youth work would be "amateurish" and not very professional; and that by funding one faith group there might be some offence caused to people of another tradition.

I certainly also found among my religious friends a degree of ignorance about what statutory bodies might need before they would help with funding and resources, even among very experienced, bright, academic and professional people.

What I learned was that if I structured a bid for financial and other help in such a way as to demonstrate that the church was first and foremost offering top-class professional youth work, with all that that entails, then suddenly there was a real willingness to help. It sounds daunting to prepare a business case, with financial forecasting, human resource management, project aims, objectives and outcomes, a support framework and exit strategy, taking account of child protection issues and insurance provision – but this is actually the "bread and butter" of many people's professional lives. Many people have these skills, from managing a budget at home, those who are unemployed and students on a tight income, through to small businesses and among people working in the public sector at all levels. All that changes is the scale and context.

During the spring of 2005 I managed to pull together enough support from the church to find sufficient volunteers to staff the Eden Bus if we could fund it. Then our local councillors, police and community representatives offered to finance a series of sessions if we would deploy the bus to the local park that was causing all the problems, and finally The Message found they had a slot in the diary when we could have the bus to come to us.

Like others who had used the Eden Bus before us, the people working on the project had a series of remarkable encounters with young people. Several years later, I still meet young adults who just want to talk about the amazing bus and the difference the people on it made to their lives. Some of the most significant meetings appeared to deny any age gap: the group of teenage girls talking to our seventy-eight-year-old grandfather about their boyfriend troubles; or the young lads wanting to get on the bus with alcohol, who were only willing to talk to women of their mum's age. Week by week we saw a change in so many young people.

Perhaps what was most remarkable, though, was the change in crime and disorder on the nights when the Eden Bus was at the park. From the very first Friday night the bus came, we saw a perceptible drop in calls to the police. There were no fewer young people about; they hadn't just moved on and started causing problems elsewhere. There was just a real drop in actual calls to the police for service. By the third week, people who didn't have a faith were talking about it being "eerie" or "spooky", because often there were no calls at all about antisocial behaviour – not one – and calls about other types of crime started to fall as well. By the time the project finished, my staff had come to expect that there would be no crime or antisocial behaviour when the bus was in town, and they knew that the effects seemed to last over the whole weekend.

When the project finished, the exit strategy was put into operation: things were going so well that we found funding for further sessions, and the work done by the bus was continued by people from the church. We continue to meet young people where they are, in the streets and the parks, as well as through some joint projects with The Message and our local authority. Crime and disorder has stayed low, the problems in that park seem a distant memory, and the area has had a period of huge regeneration with a large sports village being built, and much work done on other local amenities.

What has also come out of the Eden Bus project has been some valuable learning about what the faith community can offer to the wider community, and how to go about making that offer acceptable.

My observations are that if churches can structure offers of help (whether that is youth work, community work or anything else) in the language and format of the public sector or business world, then it has a much greater chance of being accepted. In general people seem to like people who are like them and think like them. So if "church" can learn to speak the language of the "world" it can be accepted and supported. I know this might sound obvious but I don't think it is, sometimes, especially as nowadays the perceived value of "the church" is less than it was a hundred years ago.

I would also seek to reassure people who have no faith, that working with the church is not a threatening thing. I say this especially to the police service, local authorities and other third-sector organizations. I want to highlight that most people of faith are not strange, or odd, or dangerous, and that before anything else we have the best interests of our communities at heart. By engaging with your local church to supply some much-needed youth work, and perhaps using some of your precious budget to fund it, what you can get is absolutely first-class, good-value youth work. That it also comes from a position of faith should never be ignored, because that does shape why the people are there. But it should never obscure the possibility of absolutely excellent work, in your own community, by people who live and work there and have a real passion for seeing positive change.

Appendix 2

Risk Assessment

On the following pages you can see a template for doing a risk assessment and an example. The definitions are given below:

RISK CATEGORY	Try to ensure that you highlight the risk in the most appropriate category. Some risks may appear to fit more than one category, in which case you will have to make a judgment about where to list it. Ultimately the important thing is that the risk is identified and controlled; its category is less important.
ACTIVITY	Risks associated to the specific nature of the activity being undertaken, e.g. danger of cuts using craft knives for art and craft.
ACCIDENT	Remember that the thing that defines an accident is that it is something that happens unintentionally.
INCIDENT	An incident may well involve malicious intent, although this is not necessarily the case.
ALLEGATION	Whether they turn out to be true or false, accusations are not pleasant to deal with. Your child protection policy should include methods for dealing with allegations.
HAZARD	A hazard will generally be an environmental feature that poses a risk, e.g. deep water, broken glass, or a harmful substance (such as glue).
LOCATION	Risks associated with the specific place in which the activity is being undertaken, e.g. an ice rink, the park.
COMPLAINT	The possibility that your activity may cause distress, annoyance or offence to others.
MISC.	Anything not covered in the other categories!

RISK ASSESSMENT		Activity: (insert activity)		Completed by: (insert name)		Overseen by: (insert team leader name)		
Risk category	Specific risk (describe)	Likelihood (High, Medium, Low)	Impact (High, Medium, Low)	Overall risk (Red, Amber, Green)	Control/Mitigation (describe)	Action date	Control assessment (Strong, Medium, Weak)	Actual risk (Red, Amber, Green)
Activity								
Accident								
Incident								
Allegation								
Hazard								
Location								
Complaint								
Misc.								

We used a "traffic light" system to calculate and display the risk, with "Red" meaning that there was a high level of risk, and that staff should consider whether the activity was viable, and "Green" meaning that the risk could be managed and it was all right to go ahead.

We looked at the Likelihood and Impact columns to calculate the Overall risk. "Low" + "Low" in those two columns produced "Green" in Overall risk; "High" + "High" in both produced "Red" in Overall risk. All other combinations produced "Amber". This gave an immediate idea of how much input was going to be needed in order to mitigate the risk – especially if we filled in our chart in colour.

We then looked at the effect the controls and mitigation would have: there are some things you can control well if you have put in the right amount of effort, but there are other things you can have very little effect on (see the final, very silly, example!). If these controls are suitable, you should be able to reduce the actual risk. You can see how this works in the examples below.

Risk category	Specific risk	Likelihood (High, Medium, Low)	Impact (High, Medium, Low)	Overall risk (Red, Amber, Green)	Control/Mitigation	Action date	Control assessment (Strong, Medium, Weak)	Actual risk (Red, Amber, Green)
Activity	Football injury	Medium	Medium	Amber	Referee establish firm rules and discipline	Always	Medium	Green
					Warm-up exercises	Always	Medium	
Accident	Minibus crash – injury	Low	High	Amber	Driver selection and training	(specific dates)	Strong	Green
					Regular servicing		Medium	
Incident	Violence – injuries	High	High	Red	Reschedule activity	(Date)	Medium	Green
					Ban known troublemakers	(Date)	Strong	
					Hire pro. security	(Date)	Strong	
Allegation	Assault allegation (damaging to reputation of project)	Medium	High	Amber	Conduct activities in public	Always	Strong	Green
					Work in pairs	Always	Medium	
Hazard	Broken glass – injury	High	Low	Amber	Sweep basketball court	Always	Strong	Green

Location	Ice rink – injury	Medium	Low	Amber	Higher ratio of workers	(Date)	Medium	Green
Complaint	Street noise after club	High	Medium	Amber	Talk with local residents	(Date)	Strong	Green
Misc.	Earth explodes!	Low	High	Amber	Take umbrella	Always	Weak	Amber

Other resources

If you have found this book helpful, you may also find these other resources from John Robinson useful:

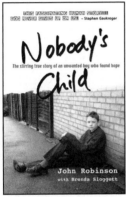

978 1 85424 623 3

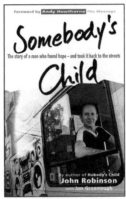

978 1 85424 852 7

Practical Christianity DVD ISBN 1-904726-59-3